# PRACTISE & PASS 11+
# VERBAL REASONING
## PRACTICE PAPERS

## Contents

⚙ Practice paper 1          3
⚙ Practice paper 2          11
⚙ Practice paper 3          19
⚙ Practice paper 4          29

---

© Peter Williams and Trotman Publishing, 2015

The right of Peter Williams to be identified as the author of this work has been asserted by him in accordance with the Copyright, Designs and Patents Act, 1988.

All rights reserved. No part of this publication may be transmitted in any form or by any means, or stored in a retrieval system without prior written permission from the publisher.

First published 2015 by Trotman Publishing, a division of Crimson Publishing Ltd, 19–21c Charles Street, Bath BA1 1HX.

ISBN 978 1 84455 430 0

A catalogue record for this book is available from the British Library.

# PRACTISE AND PASS 11+

# VERBAL REASONING
## MULTIPLE CHOICE

## PRACTICE PAPER 1

Read the following instructions carefully.

1. Do <u>not</u> begin until you are told to do so.
2. This is a multiple choice test.
3. Answers should be marked on the answer sheet provided.
4. Mark your answer in the same number on the answer sheet as the test question by drawing a firm line clearly through the rectangle next to your answer.
5. If you make a mistake, make sure you rub it out completely before putting a new answer in. There should be only one answer marked for each question, unless a question specifically tells you otherwise.
6. You may do any working out on a separate sheet of paper.
7. Make sure you keep your place on the answer sheet.
8. Work quickly and carefully. If you cannot do a question, do not waste time on it but move on to the next. If you are unsure of the answer, choose the one which you think is best.
9. You will have 50 minutes to complete this test.

## Section 1

In the questions that follow, one letter can be moved from the first word to the second word to make two new words. Only one letter must be moved and the letters cannot be rearranged in any other way. The two new words must be actual words. Find the letter that moves and mark it on your answer sheet.

**Example**    FIEND    LUNG

**Answer**    E    to form FIND and LUNGE

**1**    GLADE    HART

**2**    BRING    PLUM

**3**    ISLET    PAIN

**4**    ACRID    WINED

**5**    RAFTS    BELIES

**6**    PENDS    WINS

**7**    BRING    CHOSE

## Section 2

In the questions below, letters represent numbers. Work out the answer to each sum by replacing each letter with its corresponding number. Then find your answer and mark its letter on your answer sheet.

**Example**    If $A = 1$, $B = 2$, $C = 3$, $D = 4$ and $E = 5$, what is the answer to this sum written as a letter?
$D - B + C$

**Answer**    E (5)

**8**    If $A = 2$, $B = 3$, $C = 4$, $D = 5$ and $E = 6$, what is the answer to this sum written as a letter?
$$\frac{(A + E) \times B}{C}$$

**9**    If $A = 2$, $B = 4$, $C = 7$, $D = 8$ and $E = 58$, what is the answer to the sum $E - (C \times D)$ written as a letter?

**10**    If $A = 2$, $B = 5$, $C = 7$, $D = 8$ and $E = 20$, what is the answer to the sum $E - D - C$ written as a letter?

**11**    If $A = 4$, $B = 5$, $C = 6$, $D = 7$ and $E = 9$, what is the answer to this sum written as a letter?
$(D \times E) - (A \times C) - (C \times B)$

**12**    If $A = 3$, $B = 4$, $C = 6$, $D = 7$ and $E = 25$, what is the answer to the sum $B \times D - E$?

**13**    If $A = 11$, $B = 12$, $C = 13$, $D = 14$ and $E = 144$, what is the answer to the sum $E - (A \times B)$?

## Section 3

**14**

Tracey, Bob, Lonnie, Vicki and Maria all go shopping after work one day.
Tracey and Vicki buy rice and potatoes.
Lonnie, Tracey and Bob buy some cheese.
Maria doesn't particularly like meat but buys some ham and turkey anyway.
Lonnie and Maria buy some pasta.
Tracey buys milk but no tea.

Who buys the greatest number of items?

## Section 4

In the sentences below, a four-letter word is hidden at the end of one word and the beginning of the next word. Find the pair of words that contain the hidden word and mark the pair on your answer sheet.

**Example**    The happy pupils drew all day.

**Answer**    dre<u>w</u> <u>all</u> (the hidden word is <u>wall</u>)

**15**  She bought new pink note paper.

**16**  He tried to stifle every yawn.

**17**  The river water was lower yesterday.

**18**  We play if our parents allow.

**19**  His poor thumb endured much pain.

**20**  The coral reef ended far away.

**21**  The general ambience was very welcoming.

## Section 5

In the questions below, two words (one from each group) need to be chosen. The two words will complete their sentences in the same way. Mark <u>both</u> words on your answer sheet.

**Example**   Film is to       (watch, buy, story)
             as book is to    (paper, pen, read)

**Answer**    watch and read

22  Flow is to          (walk, run, freeze)
    as block is to      (square, bung, stone)

23  Struggle is to      (attempt, succeed, toil)
    as decide is to     (determine, think, understand)

24  Fret is to          (discuss, play, fear)
    as calm is to       (tranquil, mind, sea)

25  Anger is to         (thought, emotion, belief)
    as taste is to      (ponder, choice, sense)

26  Strain is to        (try, train, decide)
    as slight is to     (vast, light, discover)

27  Rocket is to        (moon, fuel, space)
    as submarine is to  (sink, hull, ocean)

28  Friend is to        (worker, colleague, client)
    as enemy is to      (foe, manager, organiser)

## Section 6

In the questions below, you need to find the two words which are the closest in meaning. You must choose one word from each group. Mark <u>both</u> words on your answer sheet.

**Example**

|     | rapid      | incredible | tiresome |
|     | minuscule  | quick      | slow     |

**Answer**    rapid and quick

29  traverse    reverse     diverse
    cross       search      arrive

30  desperation terror      anguish
    relaxation  worry       understanding

31  diligent    arrogant    careless
    compulsive  carefree    meticulous

32  creative    responsible ponderous
    imaginative simple      mundane

33  drowse      alert       draw
    decide      defy        snooze

34  writing     margin      journal
    border      centre      spot

35  tight       smooth      scrape
    finish      rasp        grasp

Go straight to the next section

## Section 7

In the questions below, there are five words. Three of these five words are related in some way and two are not. Find the two words which do not relate to the other three and mark them both on your answer sheet.

**Example**     colour   green   red   pink   dark

**Answer**      colour and dark

36   finish   begin   attempt   complete   conclude

37   cymbal   musical   triangle   drum   dancing

38   colon   pause   proper   apostrophe   comma

39   expensive   brooch   amulet   bracelet   silver

40   foundation   cabin   igloo   domain   ranch

41   hilarious   amusing   hysterical   explain   deliver

42   normal   extreme   customary   special   typical

## Section 8

In the sentences below, the word in CAPITAL letters is not complete. It has had three letters removed. These three letters are consecutive and spell a three-letter word. When placed back into the word in capitals it will make sense in the sentence. Find the three-letter word and mark it on your answer sheet.

**Example**    The hurt leg was wrapped in a DAGE.

**Answer**     BAN (the word in capitals should be BANDAGE)

43   The doctor told me to take my TABS.

44   I saw paper and other STATIRY on the desk.

45   We should always try to tell the TH.

46   The teacher counted SRAL new students.

47   She DLOADED the new software on her computer.

48   He SLED the pieces of paper together.

49   The next morning, the army began to ADCE.

## Section 9

Read the following information and then find the correct answer to the question and mark its letter on your answer sheet.

**50**

Vera, Colette and Jeffrey have to get to work for 9am each morning. There are two buses; the first arrives at their work place at 8.45am and the second arrives at 9.05am. Vera always gets the first bus. Colette never misses the bus she takes. Jeffrey sometimes catches the first bus and sometimes the second bus.

If the statements above are all true, which one of the statements below must also be true?

A Vera sometimes arrives late for work.
B Jeffrey is never late for work.
C Colette loves going to work.
D Jeffrey is always late for work.
E Vera sometimes catches the same bus as Jeffrey.

## Section 10

In the questions below, you need to find the letters which complete the sequence in each question. Mark the correct answer on your answer sheet. You may use the alphabet provided below to help you.

A B C D E F G H I J K L M N O P Q R S T U V W X Y Z

| **Example** | HT | IT | JU | KU | (?) |
|---|---|---|---|---|---|
| **Answer** | LV | | | | |

The first letter goes forward 1 each time and the second letter is repeated then goes forward 1.

| **51** | HG | GF | FE | ED | DC | (?) |
|---|---|---|---|---|---|---|
| **52** | JL | HN | FP | DR | BT | (?) |
| **53** | TN | TL | WQ | WO | ZT | (?) |
| **54** | VK | XL | ZH | BI | DE | (?) |
| **55** | QP | OM | MJ | KG | ID | (?) |
| **56** | DP | EO | FQ | GM | HS | (?) |
| **57** | HG | IJ | FE | KL | DC | (?) |

## Section 11

In the questions below, you need to choose one word from the top group and one word from the bottom group and combine them to form one complete, correctly spelled word. The word from the top group must always come first when the words are placed together. Mark both words on your answer sheet.

**Example**      (your    different    run)

         (turn    way    there)

**Answer**      run and way (runway)

**58**   (bar    new    this)
         (time   row    one)

**59**   (old    ran    full)
         (sack   straw  out)

**60**   (key    now    pad)
         (turn   bolt   lock)

**61**   (par    goal   ran)
         (den    in     don)

**62**   (for    more   old)
         (age    less   time)

**63**   (hard   pit    road)
         (end    her    fall)

**64**   (cob    him    garb)
         (bled   line   lean)

## Section 12

In the questions below, the three words in the second group should go together in the same way as the three words in the first group. Find the word that is missing in the second group and mark it on your answer sheet.

**Example**      BITE (BIND) WAND    FAIL (?) TOME

**Answer**      FAME

**65**   SHIP (FLIP) FLAN    SAND (?) WIFE

**66**   WEST (WAIT) RAIN    TURN (?) PORE

**67**   FILE (FLOP) SOUP    SANE (?) LIMP

**68**   SPOT (PANT) MANE    CLOG (?) TUNE

**69**   BORE (READ) DANK    DASH (?) WORE

**70**   FEAR (LIFE) SOIL    PEEL (?) HAIR

**71**   VILE (SLIP) SPAN    KNOW (?) LEAP

## Section 13

In each question below, find the number that continues the series in the most sensible way and mark it on your answer sheet.

**Example**     3     6     9     12     15     ?

**Answer**     18

**72**     32     26     22     20     16     ?

**73**     5     7     11     19     35     ?

**74**     3     9     8     14     13     ?

**75**     9     14     8     18     7     ?

**76**     −3     1     0     4     3     ?

**77**     3     4     7     11     18     ?

**78**     3     4     6     8     12     ?

## Section 14

A B C D E F G H I J K L M N O P Q R S T U V W X Y Z

In the questions below, use the alphabet above to help you work out the answers. Work out the letter or letters that will complete each sequence in the best way and mark your answer on your answer sheet.

**Example**     AB is to DE as KL is to ?

**Answer**     NO

**79**     AZ is to DW as FU is to ?

**80**     DB is to GI as OM is to ?

**81**     NM is to KJ as CB is to ?

**82**     LO is to MN as CF is to ?

**83**     JK is to IL as QR is to ?

**84**     UR is to PM as GD is to ?

**85**     SQ is to RT as EC is to ?

# PRACTISE & PASS 11+

# VERBAL REASONING
## MULTIPLE CHOICE

### PRACTICE PAPER 2

Read the following instructions carefully.

1. Do not begin until you are told to do so.
2. This is a multiple choice test.
3. Answers should be marked on the answer sheet provided.
4. Mark your answer in the same number on the answer sheet as the test question by drawing a firm line clearly through the rectangle next to your answer.
5. If you make a mistake, make sure you rub it out completely before putting a new answer in. There should be only one answer marked for each question, unless a question specifically tells you otherwise.
6. You may do any working out on a separate sheet of paper.
7. Make sure you keep your place on the answer sheet.
8. Work quickly and carefully. If you cannot do a question, do not waste time on it but move on to the next. If you are unsure of the answer, choose the one which you think is best.
9. You will have 50 minutes to complete this test.

## Section 1

In the questions that follow, one letter can be moved from the first word to the second word to make two new words. Only one letter must be moved and the letters cannot be rearranged in any other way. The two new words must be actual words. Find the letter that moves and mark it on your answer sheet.

**Example**     GREED   THIN

**Answer**     <u>G</u>     REED     THING

**1**   SURGE     RIDS

**2**   THUMP     SALE

**3**   GUILT     ANT

**4**   GLAND     SLUG

**5**   RANGE     RISE

**6**   CRAMP     PITH

**7**   SWAMP     STALE

## Section 2

In the questions below, there are five words. Three of these five words are related in some way and two are not. Find the two words which do not relate to the other three and mark them <u>both</u> on your answer sheet.

**Example**     high   lofty   interesting   elevated   short

**Answer**     interesting and short

**8**   view   arrive   vista   watch   scene

**9**   china   plate   metal   wood   strong

**10**  smooth   level   rotor   rough   deed

**11**  ruby   pearl   jade   money   price

**12**  hike   visit   park   meadow   dale

**13**  comb   loft   watch   seek   search

**14**  vole   mouse   gerbil   wasp   mammal

## Section 3

In the questions below, letters represent numbers. Work out the answer to each sum by replacing each letter with its corresponding number. Then find your answer and mark its letter on your answer sheet.

**Example**   If A = 1, B = 2, C = 3, D = 4 and E = 8, what is the answer to this sum written as a letter?
$$E - D - A$$

**Answer**    C (3)

**15** If A = 2, B = 3, C = 4, D = 8 and E = 12, what is the answer to this sum written as a letter?
$$\frac{(C + E) \times A}{C}$$

**16** If A = 3, B = 4, C = 6, D = 8 and E = 12, what is the answer to the sum (C × D) ÷ (A × B) written as a letter?

**17** If A = 2, B = 3, C = 9, D = 8 and E = 24, what is the answer to the sum E ÷ D + (A × B) written as a letter?

**18** If A = 3, B = 6, C = 7, D = 9 and E = 15, what is the answer to the sum (E + B) × A ÷ D written as a letter?

**19** If A = 3, B = 4, C = 5, D = 12 and E = 48, what is the answer to this sum written as a letter?
$$\frac{A \times B \times C}{D}$$

**20** If A = 11, B = 12, C = 13, D = 14 and E = 25, what is the answer to the sum (D × B) − (A × C) written as a letter?

**21** If A = 10, B = 12, C = 15, D = 20 and E = 25, what is the answer to the sum (B × E) ÷ D written as a letter?

## Section 4

**22**

Five children sit in a row in class. Jo sits next to John. Gayle sits next but one to John but not next to Kevin. Prabal sits on one end of the row and Kevin sits next to him.
Who sits in the middle of the row?

## Section 5

In the questions below, two words (one from each group) need to be chosen. The two words will complete their sentences in the same way. Mark both words on your answer sheet.

**Example**    sandwich is to    (smell, buy, eat)
               as coffee is to   (cup, drink, grind)

**Answer**     eat and drink

**23**  went is to           (walk, go, run)
        as took is to        (bring, brought, take)

**24**  brake is to          (rapid, destroy, bake)
        as drive is to       (car, dive, engine)

**25**  feeble is to         (courage, calm, weak)
        as painful is to     (hurtful, medicine, healed)

**26**  rotate is to         (chair, window, wheel)
        as elevate is to     (door, lift, radiator)

**27**  camp is to           (burn, palm, barracks)
        as step is to        (pest, pace, ramp)

**28**  vast is to           (tiny, board, planet)
        as minuscule is to   (thin, huge, minute)

**29**  claim is to          (write, discover, stake)
        as flail is to       (struggle, lose, touch)

## Section 6

In the questions below, you need to choose one word from the top group and one word from the bottom group and combine them to form one complete, correctly spelled word. The word from the top group must always come first when the words are placed together. Mark both words on your answer sheet.

**Example**   (sauce   pan    nice)
              (hot     food   cake)

**Answer**    pan and cake (pancake)

**30**  (sit    bit    next)
        (one    down   ten)

**31**  (eye    bird   ear)
        (see    hear   nest)

**32**  (fresh  cold   imp)
        (air    now    lie)

**33**  (wood   rib    gold)
        (bar    den    cage)

**34**  (awe    our    find)
        (some   loss   time)

**35**  (cask   hob    sea)
        (bled   it     saw)

**36**  (so     are    err)
        (then   if     and)

## Section 7

In the sentences below, a four-letter word is hidden at the end of one word and the beginning of the next word. Find the pair of words that contain the hidden word and mark them on your answer sheet.

**Example**   The farmer caught all his animals.

**Answer**    caugh<u>t all</u> (the hidden word is <u>tall</u>)

**37**   Her coat hung on the peg.

**38**   We should wash our hands properly.

**39**   He stood up and leaned over.

**40**   The golfer needed to play well.

**41**   They stared as the ogre approached!

**42**   The beautiful lamb nibbled fresh grass.

**43**   She occasionally earns money during weekends.

## Section 8

**44**

Patrick, Zoe and Bruce take their driving test. They must score above 80% to pass the test. Zoe scores 83% and Bruce scores 80%. Patrick scores less then Zoe.

Using the above information, only one of the statements below must be true. Which one?

A   All three passed their driving test.
B   Patrick had the lowest score.
C   Only Zoe passed the driving test.
D   Bruce did not pass the driving test.
E   Zoe and Patrick passed the driving test.

## Section 9

In the sentences below, the word in CAPITAL letters is not complete. It has had three letters removed. These three letters are consecutive and spell a three-letter word. When placed back into the word in capitals it will make sense in the sentence. Find the three-letter word and mark it on your answer sheet.

**Example**  The mechanic REPED the car.

**Answer**  AIR (the word in capitals should be REPAIRED)

**45**  They used lovely INGIENTS in the cake.

**46**  The film star signed AUTOGHS for his fans.

**47**  Everyone gasped as they watched the circus ACAT.

**48**  The girl RCHED everywhere for her missing cat.

**49**  The room looked lovely once it had been DECOED.

**50**  The famous ARCECT designed an amazing building.

**51**  The beautiful sunrise was truly MAGNIFNT.

## Section 10

In the questions below, you need to find the two words which are the closest in meaning. You must choose one word from each group. Mark <u>both</u> words on your answer sheet.

**Example**   huge    interesting   quiet
              tiny    thin          vast

**Answer**    huge and vast

**52**  carcass    cutlass      erode
        monstrous  corpse       grief

**53**  carefree   impulsive    loyal
        faithful   thoughtless  pensive

**54**  slovenly   intriguing   industrious
        spectacular sparse      hardworking

**55**  direct     remarkable   deliberate
        discuss    accidental   certain

**56**  vent       elevator     aisle
        duct       shoot        barrier

**57**  image      visage       phantom
        ghost      shadow       scared

**58**  follow     mountain     discover
        trail      outside      mystery

## Section 11

In the questions below, you need to find the letters which complete the sequence in each question. Mark the correct answer on your answer sheet. You may use the alphabet provided below to help you.

A B C D E F G H I J K L M N O P Q R S T U V W X Y Z

**Example**    PM    QM    RL    SL    (?)

**Answer**    TK

The first letter goes forward one place each time and the second letter is repeated and then goes back one place.

**59**    DE    GH    FG    IJ    HI    (?)

**60**    PD    OE    MG    JJ    FN    (?)

**61**    FV    KT    OR    RP    TN    (?)

**62**    BY    DW    FU    HS    JQ    (?)

**63**    CB    MN    BA    NO    AZ    OP    (?)

**64**    LM    KN    JO    IP    HQ    (?)

**65**    QX    NU    MT    JQ    IP    (?)

## Section 12

In the questions below, the three words in the second group should go together in the same way as the three words in the first group. Find the word that is missing in the second group and mark it on your answer sheet.

**Example**    WIFE (WING) BANG    THIS (?) GLEN

**Answer**    THEN

**66**    LEAF (FARE) TIER    GRAB (?) HEEL

**67**    WIRE (BIRD) DAUB    CURE (?) EVIL

**68**    ARCH (PACE) STEP    CLAP (?) FIRS

**69**    LIVE (VINE) VENT    CORE (?) DIVE

**70**    CYAN (MANY) CALM    DART (?) BOAR

**71**    FATE (LOAF) COAL    ENVY (?) HURT

**72**    CLIP (PACT) TEAR    WITH (?) LION

## Section 13

In each question below, find the number that continues the series in the most sensible way and mark it on your answer sheet.

**Example**   3   6   9   12   (?)

**Answer**   15

**73**   2   6   18   54   (?)

**74**   37   17   32   21   27   (?)

**75**   19   2   17   3   14   (?)

**76**   64   32   16   8   4   (?)

**77**   41   14   63   36   85   (?)

**78**   4   7   11   18   29   (?)

**79**   2   4   3   9   4   (?)

## Section 14

A B C D E F G H I J K L M N O P Q R S T U V W X Y Z

In the questions below, use the alphabet above to help you work out the answers. Work out each code for each question and mark your answer on your answer sheet. There is a different code for each question.

**Example**   If the code for EYE is DXD, what is the code for NOSE?

**Answer**   MNRD

**80**   If the code for NAIL is PCKN, what is the code for SCREW?

**81**   If the code for BREAD is YOBXA, what is the code for SLICE?

**82**   If the code for GLASS is HNDWX, what is the code for JUICE?

**83**   If the code for DREAM is ESFBN, what does OJHIU mean?

**84**   If the code for TORNADO is SPPPXGK, what is the code for TYPHOON?

**85**   If the code for BRUSH is DTWUJ, what does RCKPV mean?

# PRACTISE & PASS 11+

# VERBAL REASONING
## MULTIPLE CHOICE

## PRACTICE PAPER 3

Read the following instructions carefully.

1. Do not begin until you are told to do so.

2. This is a multiple choice test.

3. Answers should be marked on the answer sheet provided.

4. Mark your answer in the same number on the answer sheet as the test question by drawing a firm line clearly through the rectangle next to your answer.

5. If you make a mistake, make sure you rub it out completely before putting a new answer in. There should be only one answer marked for each question, unless a question specifically tells you otherwise.

6. You may do any working out on a separate sheet of paper.

7. Make sure you keep your place on the answer sheet.

8. Work quickly and carefully. If you cannot do a question, do not waste time on it but move on to the next. If you are unsure of the answer, choose the one which you think is best.

9. You will have 50 minutes to complete this test.

## Section 1

In the questions that follow, one letter can be moved from the first word to the second word to make two new words. Only one letter must be moved and the letters cannot be rearranged in any other way. The two new words must be actual words. Find the letter that moves and mark it on your answer sheet.

**Example**  GLOBE  RIPE

**Answer**  G  LOBE  GRIPE

1. GRASP  GAPE
2. FLAME  STILE
3. LATHE  SORT
4. BLEAT  GRAVE
5. SINGE  SPAR
6. PURGE  CRAM
7. HALVE  VALE

## Section 2

In the questions below, there are five words. Three of these five words are related in some way and two are not. Find the two words which do not relate to the other three and mark them both on your answer sheet.

**Example**  cherry  apple  garden  orange  tasty

**Answer**  garden and tasty

8. curious  inquisitive  interested  boring  tedious
9. grove  route  thicket  mountain  copse
10. parallel  accurate  lopsided  irregular  crooked
11. escape  capture  dodge  deluge  elude
12. dull  polished  cracked  burnished  varnished
13. learned  petulant  sage  wise  practice
14. topical  rainforest  current  recent  warm

## Section 3

In the questions below, letters represent numbers. Work out the answer to each sum by replacing each letter with its corresponding number. Then find your answer and mark its letter on your answer sheet.

**Example**   If A = 1, B = 2, C = 3, D = 4 and E = 5, what is the answer to this sum written as a letter?
E + B − D

**Answer**   C (3)

**15**   If A = 3, B = 5, C = 7, D = 9 and E = 62, what is the answer to the sum AD + BC written as a letter?

**16**   If A = 2, B = 4, C = 6, D = 8 and E = 10, what is the answer to the sum (B + C + D) − (A + E) written as a letter?

**17**   If A = 2, B = 5, C = 7, D = 10 and E = 15, what is the answer to the sum BC − AD written as a letter?

**18**   If A = 2, B = 5, C = 7, D = 9 and E = 8, what is the answer to this sum written as a letter?
CE − BD − A

**19**   If A = 2, B = 7, C = 10, D = 17 and E = 25, what is the answer to this sum written as a letter?
$$\frac{(A + C) \times B}{D + E}$$

**20**   If A = 28, B = 12, C = 13, D = 14 and E = 50, what is the answer to the sum (D × E) ÷ (B + C) written as a letter?

**21**   If A = 2, B = 3, C = 5, D = 6 and E = 9, what is the answer to this sum written as a letter?
$$\frac{D + E}{C}$$

## Section 4

**22**

Eric and Ram wear orange shorts, Saffron and Rolf do not.
Rolf and Ram wear red scarves, the others wear blue.
Eric and Saffron wear black shoes, the others do not.
Claire wears a green hat.
If the information above is all true then which one statement below must also be true?

A   Saffron has black shoes and a red scarf.
B   Eric wears orange shorts and a blue scarf.
C   Ram wears orange shorts and black shoes.
D   Rolf does not have black shoes but wears a red scarf and orange shorts.
E   Claire loves wearing clothes.

## Section 5

In the questions below, two words (one from each group) need to be chosen. The two words will complete their sentences in the same way. Mark both words on your answer sheet.

**Example**  Apple is to  (eat, fruit, tree)
 as chicken is to (fly, drink, meat)

**Answer**  fruit and meat

**23** Trip is to (remain, stumble, hotel)
 as gather is to (divide, shop, collect)

**24** Nurse is to (care, hospital, ill)
 as teacher is to (playground, understand, instruct)

**25** Envelope is to (stamp, delivery, letter)
 as bag is to (carry, shopping, plastic)

**26** Nail is to (hammer, finger, fix)
 as button is to (blouse, round, small)

**27** Explore is to (pioneer, jungle, rocket)
 as repair is to (replace, mechanic, tools)

**28** Dice are to (game, roll, numbers)
 as cards are to (shuffle, stack, pack)

**29** Paint is to (decorate, brush, colour)
 as chop is to (axe, swing, woods)

## Section 6

**30**

Lola is a third of the age of Edward who is 5 years older than Craig.
Craig's sister Wendola is 2 years older than her brother and will be 16 next year.

If the information above is correct, which one statement below must also be true?

A  Edward is the youngest.
B  Lola is 27.
C  Craig is 10 years older than Lola.
D  Edward is older than Wendola.
E  Craig is the oldest.

## Section 7

In the questions below, you need to choose one word from the top group and one word from the bottom group and combine them to form one complete, correctly spelled word. The word from the top group must always come first when the words are placed together. Mark <u>both</u> words on your answer sheet.

**Example**    (light    heavy    large)
                (time    house    carry)

**Answer**    light and house (lighthouse)

**31**    (piece    pill    set)
          (it    tee    low)

**32**    (mode    most    long)
          (rate    time    lea)

**33**    (duck    nice    goose)
          (bird    feather    berry)

**34**    (either    vend    and)
          (or    one    soon)

**35**    (main    old    man)
          (part    ace    age)

**36**    (car    deep    new)
          (pit    down    pet)

**37**    (ban    hid    cord)
          (den    done    string)

## Section 8

A B C D E F G H I J K L M N O P Q R S T U V W X Y Z

In the questions below, use the alphabet above to help you work out the answers. Work out the letter or letters that will complete each sequence in the best way and mark your answer on your answer sheet.

**Example**    KL is to OP as ST is to ?

**Answer**    WX

The first letter goes forward four places and the second letter also goes forward four places.

**38**    AC is to ZB as GI is to ?

**39**    RQ is to TU as ML is to ?

**40**    HK is to IM as TW is to ?

**41**    FD is to EG as YW is to ?

**42**    FH is to JD as RT is to ?

**43**    BE is to YV as GJ is to?

**44**    CD is to WX as FG is to ?

## Section 9

In the sentences below, the word in CAPITAL letters is not complete. It has had three letters removed. These three letters are consecutive and spell a three-letter word. When placed back into the word in capitals it will make sense in the sentence. Find the three-letter word and mark it on your answer sheet.

**Example**     She CTED happily on the telephone.

**Answer**      HAT (the word in capitals should be CHATTED)

**45**  Three CANATES applied for the job.

**46**  The runner trained every day for the MAHON.

**47**  The ducks WLED down to the river.

**48**  The morning sunrise looked REY beautiful.

**49**  The children made planes by FING pieces of paper.

**50**  The brave knight wore a suit of metal ARM.

**51**  The thief ILY left the scene of the crime.

## Section 10

In the questions below, you need to find the two words which are closest in meaning. You must choose one word from each group. Mark <u>both</u> words on your answer sheet.

**Example**     (simple, tricky, obvious)
                (strange, plain, interesting)

**Answer**      simple and plain

**52**  (grave, whole, comical)
        (unsure, graceful, serious)

**53**  (discussion, decision, thought)
        (debate, influence, hesitation)

**54**  (imitation, authentic, replica)
        (genuine, intricate, peculiar)

**55**  (description, impression, episode)
        (edition, account, revision)

**56**  (poster, diary, booklet)
        (pamphlet, reference, design)

**57**  (note, evidence, investigation)
        (solution, thought, proof)

**58**  (robust, brave, thoughtless)
        (valiant, vibrant, victorious)

## Section 11

In the sentences below, a four-letter word is hidden at the end of one word and the beginning of the next word. Find the pair of words that contain the hidden word and mark the pair on your answer sheet.

**Example**     He hurt his wrist and arm.

**Answer**      hurt his (the hidden word is this)

**59**  The chef happily cooked us kippers.

**60**  His wife chose sumptuous new carpets.

**61**  The witch opened her potion book.

**62**  The super hero grew even stronger!

**63**  She gently bandaged the damaged ankle.

**64**  They did not swap luggage labels.

**65**  Both issues of the paper sold.

## Section 12

In the questions below, the three words in the second group should go together in the same way as the three words in the first group. Find the word that is missing in the second group and mark it on your answer sheet.

**Example**     KIND (KITE) GATE        HALT (?) RUNG

**Answer**      HANG

**66**  FIRE (FIST) CAST        BOTH (?) CANE

**67**  VALE (VOTE) NOTE        LICK (?) SURE

**68**  SORE (SOLE) SILK        PACY (?) BIBS

**69**  CASK (SCAR) DRAW        ROPE (?) EMIT

**70**  SWAP (WINS) NAIL        SHIP (?) PLOY

**71**  COPE (POKE) LIKE        SANG (?) LOPE

**72**  GRID (GOLD) GLOW        BEND (?) TRIP

## Section 13

In each question below, find the number that continues the series in the most sensible way and mark it on your answer sheet.

**Example**     5     10     15     20     ?

**Answer**     25

**73**  23  17  19  21  15  ?

**74**  2  6  18  54  162  ?

**75**  72  36  18  9  4.5  ?

**76**  6  16  161  1161  11611  ?

**77**  0.15  0.3  0.45  0.6  0.75  ?

## Section 14

In the questions below, the three numbers in each group are related in the same way. Find the number which completes the final group and mark it on your answer sheet.

**Example**     (5 [15] 3)     (2 [16] 8)     (7 [?] 4)

**Answer**     28 (7 × 4)

**78**  (7 [19] 5)     (4 [19] 11)     (8 [?] 9)

**79**  (3 [28] 9)     (5 [21] 4)     (8 [?] 3)

**80**  (14 [20] 26)   (4 [9] 14)     (7 [?] 25)

**81**  (6 [8] 24)     (5 [14] 35)    (4 [?] 32)

**82**  (12 [9] 15)    (5 [15] 40)    (7 [?] 17)

## Section 15

Below are five words and three number codes. Each number code represents one of the words. Two words will have no code. First work out which word each number code represents then use the information to answer the questions that follow.

**Example**  REACH  CRATE  CAMEL  LURCH  RIVAL
47862  83162  68193

**Answer**  REACH = 83162   LURCH = 47862
CRATE = 68193

CAROL   FLOAT   FIRST   FOCUS   DRIFT

37269   32185   16427

**83** Find the code for the word COAST.

**84** Find the code for the word ACTOR.

**85** Find the word which 36879 stands for.

**END OF TEST – PLEASE CHECK ALL YOUR ANSWERS**

# PRACTISE & PASS 11+

# VERBAL REASONING
## MULTIPLE CHOICE

## PRACTICE PAPER 4

Read the following instructions carefully.

1. Do not begin until you are told to do so.
2. This is a multiple choice test.
3. Answers should be marked on the answer sheet provided.
4. Mark your answer in the same number on the answer sheet as the test question by drawing a firm line clearly through the rectangle next to your answer.
5. If you make a mistake, make sure you rub it out completely before putting a new answer in. There should be only one answer marked for each question, unless a question specifically tells you otherwise.
6. You may do any working out on a separate sheet of paper.
7. Make sure you keep your place on the answer sheet.
8. Work quickly and carefully. If you cannot do a question, do not waste time on it but move on to the next. If you are unsure of the answer, choose the one which you think is best.
9. You will have 50 minutes to complete this test.

## Section 1

In the questions below, there are five words. Three of these five words are related in some way and two are not. Find the two words which do not relate to the other three and mark them both on your answer sheet.

**Example**   lung   heart   human   liver   body

**Answer**   human and body

**1**   screech   beak   scrabble   scrape   talon

**2**   uncomfortable   relaxed   tense   cramped   gentle

**3**   upbeat   miserable   diseased   downbeat   glum

**4**   disaster   saviour   awesome   cataclysm   tragedy

**5**   handle   terminal   lever   circuit   hilt

**6**   conserve   alter   modify   adjust   agree

**7**   cement   demand   secure   enquire   fuse

## Section 2

In the questions below, letters represent numbers. Work out the answer to each sum by replacing each letter with its corresponding number. Then find your answer and mark its letter on your answer sheet.

**Example**   If $A = 1$, $B = 2$, $C = 3$, $D = 4$ and $E = 5$, what is the answer to this sum written as a letter?
$E + B - D$

**Answer**   C (3)

**8**   If $A = 3$, $B = 5$, $C = 7$, $D = 9$ and $E = 29$, what is the answer to this sum written as a letter?
$(A \times D) - B + C$

**9**   If $A = 2$, $B = 4$, $C = 8$, $D = 20$ and $E = 10$, what is the answer to this sum written as a letter?
$(E \div B) \times C$

**10**   If $A = 2$, $B = 5$, $C = 7$, $D = 10$ and $E = 15$, what is the answer to this sum written as a letter?
$(D + E) \div B + A$

**11**   If $A = 2$, $B = 5$, $C = 7$, $D = 9$ and $E = 8$, what is the answer to this sum written as a letter?
$B - C + (A \times E) - D$

**12**   If $A = 2$, $B = 4$, $C = 18$, $D = 16$ and $E = 25$, what is the answer to this sum written as a letter?
$$\frac{(E - D) \times B}{C \div A}$$

Go straight to the next section

Go straight to the next section

## Section 3

**13**

Cary, Rick, Basil, Ellie and Fahana went to the fun fair.
Cary went on the Big Wheel.
Rick and Ellie went on the Ghost Train.
Only Cary and Rick did not go on the Dodgems.
Fahana and Basil went on the Roller Coaster.
Only Rick and Basil didn't go on the Waltzer.

If the information above is all true then who went on the fewest rides?

A   Cary
B   Rick
C   Basil
D   Ellie
E   Fahana

## Section 4

In the questions below, two words (one from each group) need to be chosen. The two words will complete their sentences in the same way. Mark both words on your answer sheet.

**Example**   violin is to       (squeak, play, strings)
              as trumpet is to   (blow, brass, loud)

**Answer**    strings and brass

**14**  Fear is to         (fright, emotion, haunted)
        as envy is to      (desire, need, scared)

**15**  Ride is to         (watch, balance, dire)
        as life is to      (years, file, live)

**16**  Glacier is to      (massive, ice, mountain)
        as geyser is to    (water, fire, rocks)

**17**  Embark is to       (arrive, seek, cover)
        as deliver is to   (send, dispatch, correspond)

**18**  Browse is to       (think, search, ignore)
        as catalogue is to (order, magazine, paper)

## Section 5

**19**

Lance, Gael, Daria, Matt and Tina all go to extra lessons after school.
Matt goes to all the lessons that do not involve music.
Daria, Lance and Tina go to geography on Mondays.
All the children except Daria go to painting on Thursdays.
Gael and Lance are the only ones to go to dance on Tuesdays.
Gael and Tina go to ancient history on a Wednesday.
Matt goes to cycling.

If the information above is all correct, who attends the most extra lessons?

A   Lance
B   Gael
C   Daria
D   Matt
E   Tina

## Section 6

In the questions below, you need to choose one word from the top group and one word from the bottom group which combine to form one complete, correctly spelled word. The word from the top group must always come first when the words are placed together. Mark <u>both</u> words on your answer sheet.

**Example**     (really   born   care)
                (full     well   free)

**Answer**      care and free (carefree)

**20**   (across   crest   bad)
         (fallen   time    there)

**21**   (deep     imp     go)
         (down     art     lend)

**22**   (was      has     have)
         (ten      been    lost)

**23**   (door     old     candid)
         (ate      place   mouse)

**24**   (van      car     bus)
         (door     guard   lane)

## Section 7

A B C D E F G H I J K L M N O P Q R S T U V W X Y Z

In the questions below, use the alphabet above to help you work out the answers. Work out the letter or letters that will complete each sequence in the best way and mark your answer on your answer sheet.

**Example**     NI is to KL as WR is to ?

**Answer**     TU
The first letter goes back three places and the second letter goes forward three places.

**25**     FD is to CA as NL is to ?

**26**     MP is to TW as EH is to ?

**27**     QP is to TM as KJ is to ?

**28**     CA is to WV as SQ is to ?

**29**     SP is to IK as UR is to ?

## Section 8

In the sentences below, the word in CAPITAL letters is not complete. It has had three letters removed. These three letters are consecutive and spell a three-letter word. When placed back into the word in capitals it will make sense in the sentence. Find the three-letter word and mark it on your answer sheet.

**Example**     He SPED on the icy pavement.

**Answer**     LIP (the word in capitals should be SLIPPED)

**30**     The crocodile DEVED its prey.

**31**     He got drenched in a DPOUR of rain.

**32**     It took a while but he FINY passed his test.

**33**     The old vase was extremely DELIE.

**34**     The actors gave a simply wonderful PERFORCE.

## Section 9

In the questions below, you need to find the two words which are closest in meaning. You must choose one word from each group. Mark <u>both</u> words on your answer sheet.

**Example**  (awkward, simple, strange)
(plain, interesting, idea)

**Answer**  simple and plain

**35** (fraction, attempt, victor)
(race, winner, third)

**36** (creative, formal, ordinary)
(natural, standard, careful)

**37** (partial, complete, unfinished)
(comprehensive, apprehensive, unsure)

**38** (cable, string, stretch)
(electric, knot, wire)

**39** (harm, treat, medicine)
(heal, injure, hospital)

## Section 10

In the sentences below, a four-letter word is hidden at the end of one word and the beginning of the next word. Find the pair of words that contain the hidden word and mark the pair on your answer sheet.

**Example**  The people adored dancing and singing.

**Answer**  peo<u>ple</u> <u>ad</u>ored (plea or lead)

**40** The bee hive started to vibrate.

**41** The skate rink now opens daily.

**42** The pale aqua yacht sailed away.

**43** Our young librarian is really helpful.

**44** They listened as the teacher explained.

## Section 11

In the questions below, the three words in the second group should go together in the same way as the three words in the first group. Find the word that is missing in the second group and mark it on your answer sheet.

**Example**  BUT (BAD) HAD    SAW (?) DIP

**Answer**  SIP

**45** DEN (NET) ATE    DRY (?) AWE

**46** VAT (TAR) TRY    SIN (?) ELK

**47** PURE (RIPE) VEIN    CUPS (?) CYAN

**48** FLAT (FEAT) TALE    CLAN (?) FISH

**49** BIRD (DIRE) HEIR    HUNT (?) MEAN

**50** STORM (MOAN) SNARE    CLAMP (?) STRUM

**51** FABLE (BARN) RANGE    LEVEL (?) NOTES

## Section 12

In each question below, find the number that continues the series in the most sensible way and mark it on your answer sheet.

**Example**  4  8  12  16  ?

**Answer**  20

**52**  57  49  50  56  43  ?

**53**  2.9  2.91  3.91  3.92  4.92  ?

**54**  3  4  6  9  13  ?

**55**  3888  648  108  18  ?

**56**  12  16  25  41  66  ?

**57**  2  1  3  4  7  ?

## Section 13

In the questions below, the three numbers in each group are related in the same way. Find the number which completes the final group and mark it on your answer sheet.

**Example**    (4 [10] 6)    (5 [14] 9)    (8 [?] 14)

**Answer**    22 (8+14)

**58**    (35 [10] 7)    (24 [6] 8)    (72 [?] 9)

**59**    (17 [38] 2)    (13 [36] 5)    (16 [?] 4)

**60**    (5 [31] 6)    (3 [28] 9)    (7 [?] 8)

**61**    (13 [21] 4)    (15 [21] 3)    (14 [?] 7)

**62**    (12 [9] 24)    (15 [11] 29)    (22 [?] 38)

## Section 14

Below are four words and three number codes. Each number code represents one of the words. One word will have no code. First-work out which word each number code represents then use the information to answer the questions that follow.

**Example**    HOIST    HOTEL    STOLE    LITHE

57381    93718    82791

**Answer**    STOLE = 57381    HOTEL = 93718
LITHE = 82791

SLICE    VITAL    LIVES    SLEPT

25169    53812    83975

**63**    Find the code for the word PETAL.

**64**    Find the code for the word STAVE.

**65**    Find the word which 65791 stands for.

## Section 15

Below are four words and three number codes. Each number code represents one of the words. One word will have no code. First work out which word each number code represents then use the information to answer the questions that follow.

**Example**      HOIST     HOTEL     STOLE     LITHE

                 57381     93718     82791

**Answer**     STOLE = 57381    HOTEL = 93718
               LITHE = 82791

STAMP     PEARL     GRANT     GLEAM

17493     23748     56481

**66** Find the word which 29417 stands for.

**67** Find the word which 14275 stands for.

**68** Find the code for the word AMPLE.

## Section 16

In the questions below, you need to find the two words which are the most opposite in meaning. You must choose one word from each group. Mark both words on your answer sheet.

**Example**      (above, near, around)
                 (close, below, over)

**Answer**       above and below

**69** (expensive, expand, experience)
     (contract, dear, constant)

**70** (vigour, nimble, dexterity)
     (energy, skill, lethargy)

**71** (difficult, genuine, ruthless)
     (merciful, confused, catastrophic)

**72** (interrogate, deviate, aggravate)
     (intensify, soothe, demand)

**73** (eliminate, luminous, elevate)
     (disqualify, dark, hoist)

## Section 17

These questions contain three pairs of words. Find the word that completes the last pair of words <u>in the same way</u> as the other two pairs and mark it on your answer sheet.

**Example**  (chair   hair)   (spine   pine)   (glean   ?)

**Answer**  lean

**74**  (drink   ride)   (clamp   lace)   (grave   ?)

**75**  (lemons   mole)   (remote   more)   (invade   ?)

**76**  (dapple   dale)   (fiddle   file)   (divert   ?)

**77**  (people   pole)   (gleams   gems)   (chants   ?)

**78**  (mettle   met)   (settle   set)   (towers   ?)

## Section 18

A B C D E F G H I J K L M N O P Q R S T U V W X Y Z

In the questions below, use the alphabet above to help you work out the answers. Work out the letter or letters that will complete each sequence in the best way and mark your answer on your answer sheet.

**Example**   KJ   LI   MH   NG   ?

**Answer**   OF
The first letter goes forward one place and the second letter goes back one place.

**79**   CX   EV   GT   IR   ?

**80**   KL   PN   TQ   WU   ?

**81**   HD   GE   EG   AH   ?

**82**   NC   MC   LE   KE   ?

**83**   NM   OP   LK   QR   ?

**84**   TV   QX   NZ   KB   ?

**85**   XQ   VR   UT   SU   RW   ?

# PRACTISE & PASS 11+

# VERBAL REASONING
## ANSWER GRIDS

Students should mark their answers to the practice papers in this answer booklet.

## Contents

| | |
|---|---|
| Practice Paper 1 | 2 |
| Practice Paper 2 | 7 |
| Practice Paper 3 | 12 |
| Practice Paper 4 | 17 |

---

© Peter Williams and Trotman Publishing, 2015

The right of Peter Williams to be identified as the author of this work has been asserted by him in accordance with the Copyright, Designs and Patents Act, 1988.

All rights reserved. No part of this publication may be transmitted in any form or by any means, or stored in a retrieval system without prior written permission from the publisher.

First published 2015 by Trotman Publishing, a division of Crimson Publishing Ltd, 19–21c Charles Street, Bath BA1 1HX.

ISBN 978 1 84455 430 0

A catalogue record for this book is available from the British Library.

# PRACTICE PAPER 1

Student's name

School name

Date of test

**Please mark answers like this** ⊟

## Section 1

| EXAMPLE | 1 | 2 | 3 | 4 | 5 | 6 | 7 |
|---|---|---|---|---|---|---|---|
| F | G | B | I | A | R | P | B |
| I | L | R | S | C | A | E | R |
| E | A | I | L | R | F | N | I |
| N | D | N | E | I | T | D | N |
| D | E | G | T | D | S | S | G |

## Section 2

| EXAMPLE | 8 | 9 | 10 | 11 | 12 | 13 |
|---|---|---|---|---|---|---|
| A | A | A | A | A | A | A |
| B | B | B | B | B | B | B |
| C | C | C | C | C | C | C |
| D | D | D | D | D | D | D |
| E | E | E | E | E | E | E |

## Section 3

**14**
- Tracey
- Bob
- Lonnie
- Vicki
- Maria

## Section 4

**EXAMPLE**
- The happy
- happy pupils
- pupils drew
- drew all ✓
- all day

**15**
- she bought
- bought new
- new pink
- pink note
- note paper

**16**
- he tried
- tried to
- to stifle
- stifle every
- every yawn

**17**
- the river
- river water
- water was
- was lower
- lower yesterday

**18**
- we play
- play if
- if our
- our parents
- parents allow

**19**
- his poor
- poor thumb
- thumb endured
- endured much
- much pain

**20**
- the coral
- coral reef
- reef ended
- ended far
- far away

**21**
- the general
- general ambience
- ambience was
- was very
- very welcoming

## Section 5

**EXAMPLE**
- watch = paper
- buy — pen
- story — read =

**22**
- walk — square
- run — bung
- freeze — stone

**23**
- attempt — determine
- succeed — think
- toil — understand

**24**
- discuss — tranquil
- play — mind
- fear — sea

**25**
- thought — ponder
- emotion — choice
- belief — sense

**26**
- try — vast
- train — light
- decide — discover

**27**
- moon — sink
- fuel — hull
- space — ocean

**28**
- worker — foe
- colleague — manager
- client — organiser

## Section 6

**EXAMPLE**
- rapid = minuscule
- incredible — quick =
- tiresome — slow

**29**
- traverse — cross
- reverse — search
- diverse — arrive

**30**
- desperation — relaxation
- terror — worry
- anguish — understanding

**31**
- diligent — compulsive
- arrogant — carefree
- careless — meticulous

**32**
- creative — imaginative
- responsible — simple
- ponderous — mundane

**33**
- drowse — decide
- alert — defy
- draw — snooze

**34**
- writing — border
- margin — centre
- journal — spot

**35**
- tight — finish
- smooth — rasp
- scrape — grasp

3

## Section 7

**EXAMPLE**
- colour ▪
- green ☐
- red ☐
- pink ☐
- dark ▪

**36**
- finish ☐
- begin ☐
- attempt ☐
- complete ☐
- conclude ☐

**37**
- cymbal ☐
- musical ☐
- triangle ☐
- drum ☐
- dancing ☐

**38**
- colon ☐
- pause ☐
- proper ☐
- apostrophe ☐
- comma ☐

**39**
- expensive ☐
- brooch ☐
- amulet ☐
- bracelet ☐
- silver ☐

**40**
- foundation ☐
- cabin ☐
- igloo ☐
- domain ☐
- ranch ☐

**41**
- hilarious ☐
- amusing ☐
- hysterical ☐
- explain ☐
- deliver ☐

**42**
- normal ☐
- extreme ☐
- customary ☐
- special ☐
- typical ☐

## Section 8

**EXAMPLE**
- BAN ▪
- RAT ☐
- DAM ☐
- ORE ☐
- HEN ☐

**43**
- LIT ☐
- LOT ☐
- LET ☐
- ALL ☐
- BET ☐

**44**
- OWN ☐
- AND ☐
- OUR ☐
- ONE ☐
- ANT ☐

**45**
- RUE ☐
- RUT ☐
- ROT ☐
- ROW ☐
- RUN ☐

**46**
- EVE ☐
- EAR ☐
- OUR ☐
- PEA ☐
- PET ☐

**47**
- OUR ☐
- ONE ☐
- ION ☐
- RIP ☐
- OWN ☐

**48**
- LOT ☐
- TAP ☐
- WAR ☐
- CAR ☐
- HIS ☐

**49**
- VIE ☐
- RAN ☐
- LIE ☐
- VAN ☐
- RUN ☐

## Section 9

**50**
- A ☐
- B ☐
- C ☐
- D ☐
- E ☐

## Section 10

| EXAMPLE | | 51 | | 52 | | 53 | |
|---|---|---|---|---|---|---|---|
| LV | ☰ | CB | ☐ | VZ | ☐ | ZO | ☐ |
| JK | ☐ | BC | ☐ | OZ | ☐ | ZR | ☐ |
| RQ | ☐ | AB | ☐ | AV | ☐ | BO | ☐ |
| KL | ☐ | CA | ☐ | ZV | ☐ | BT | ☐ |
| MU | ☐ | AC | ☐ | AO | ☐ | ZP | ☐ |

| 54 | | 55 | | 56 | | 57 | |
|---|---|---|---|---|---|---|---|
| EF | ☐ | GB | ☐ | JK | ☐ | KL | ☐ |
| GE | ☐ | GA | ☐ | IJ | ☐ | LM | ☐ |
| HE | ☐ | FB | ☐ | IK | ☐ | LN | ☐ |
| EG | ☐ | FA | ☐ | IS | ☐ | KM | ☐ |
| FF | ☐ | HA | ☐ | IT | ☐ | MN | ☐ |

## Section 11

| EXAMPLE | | | | 58 | | | | 59 | | | | 60 | | | |
|---|---|---|---|---|---|---|---|---|---|---|---|---|---|---|---|
| your | ☐ | turn | ☐ | bar | ☐ | time | ☐ | old | ☐ | sack | ☐ | key | ☐ | turn | ☐ |
| different | ☐ | way | ☰ | new | ☐ | row | ☐ | ran | ☐ | straw | ☐ | now | ☐ | bolt | ☐ |
| run | ☰ | there | ☐ | this | ☐ | one | ☐ | full | ☐ | out | ☐ | pad | ☐ | lock | ☐ |

| 61 | | | | 62 | | | | 63 | | | | 64 | | | |
|---|---|---|---|---|---|---|---|---|---|---|---|---|---|---|---|
| par | ☐ | den | ☐ | for | ☐ | age | ☐ | hard | ☐ | end | ☐ | cob | ☐ | bled | ☐ |
| goal | ☐ | in | ☐ | more | ☐ | less | ☐ | pit | ☐ | her | ☐ | him | ☐ | line | ☐ |
| ran | ☐ | don | ☐ | old | ☐ | time | ☐ | road | ☐ | fall | ☐ | garb | ☐ | lean | ☐ |

## Section 12

| EXAMPLE | | 65 | | 66 | | 67 | |
|---|---|---|---|---|---|---|---|
| SOME | ☐ | WINE | ☐ | PORT | ☐ | SLIP | ☐ |
| HAIL | ☐ | WIND | ☐ | PUNT | ☐ | SAME | ☐ |
| TAIL | ☐ | SANE | ☐ | TORN | ☐ | LAME | ☐ |
| FAME | ☰ | SAFE | ☐ | TORE | ☐ | SNIP | ☐ |
| RAIL | ☐ | WIFE | ☐ | PURE | ☐ | LAMP | ☐ |

| 68 | | 69 | | 70 | | 71 | |
|---|---|---|---|---|---|---|---|
| CULT | ☐ | WASH | ☐ | PAIR | ☐ | LONE | ☐ |
| CLOT | ☐ | SHOW | ☐ | HAIL | ☐ | NAPE | ☐ |
| LONE | ☐ | SORE | ☐ | PALE | ☐ | LOPE | ☐ |
| TONE | ☐ | HARE | ☐ | HALE | ☐ | KELP | ☐ |
| LUNG | ☐ | HOSE | ☐ | RIPE | ☐ | LANE | ☐ |

## Section 13

| EXAMPLE | | 72 | | 73 | | 74 | |
|---|---|---|---|---|---|---|---|
| 17 | ☐ | 14 | ☐ | 37 | ☐ | 15 | ☐ |
| 25 | ☐ | 12 | ☐ | 41 | ☐ | 17 | ☐ |
| 20 | ☐ | 10 | ☐ | 47 | ☐ | 19 | ☐ |
| 30 | ☐ | 8 | ☐ | 57 | ☐ | 21 | ☐ |
| 18 | ▭ | 6 | ☐ | 67 | ☐ | 23 | ☐ |

| 75 | | 76 | | 77 | | 78 | |
|---|---|---|---|---|---|---|---|
| 6 | ☐ | 2 | ☐ | 26 | ☐ | 15 | ☐ |
| 20 | ☐ | 4 | ☐ | 27 | ☐ | 16 | ☐ |
| 22 | ☐ | 7 | ☐ | 28 | ☐ | 20 | ☐ |
| 24 | ☐ | 8 | ☐ | 29 | ☐ | 24 | ☐ |
| 26 | ☐ | 9 | ☐ | 30 | ☐ | 30 | ☐ |

## Section 14

| EXAMPLE | | 79 | | 80 | | 81 | |
|---|---|---|---|---|---|---|---|
| LP | ☐ | IX | ☐ | RP | ☐ | FG | ☐ |
| KR | ☐ | IR | ☐ | LP | ☐ | GF | ☐ |
| NO | ▭ | CX | ☐ | LT | ☐ | ZY | ☐ |
| NP | ☐ | CR | ☐ | RT | ☐ | YZ | ☐ |
| PQ | ☐ | LR | ☐ | QT | ☐ | XZ | ☐ |

| 82 | | 83 | | 84 | | 85 | |
|---|---|---|---|---|---|---|---|
| BE | ☐ | PT | ☐ | BY | ☐ | DE | ☐ |
| BG | ☐ | PS | ☐ | YB | ☐ | BF | ☐ |
| DG | ☐ | PQ | ☐ | LI | ☐ | ED | ☐ |
| DE | ☐ | RS | ☐ | IL | ☐ | DF | ☐ |
| BH | ☐ | RT | ☐ | BX | ☐ | DG | ☐ |

# PRACTICE PAPER 2

Student's name

School name

Date of test

## Please mark answers like this ⊟

### Section 1

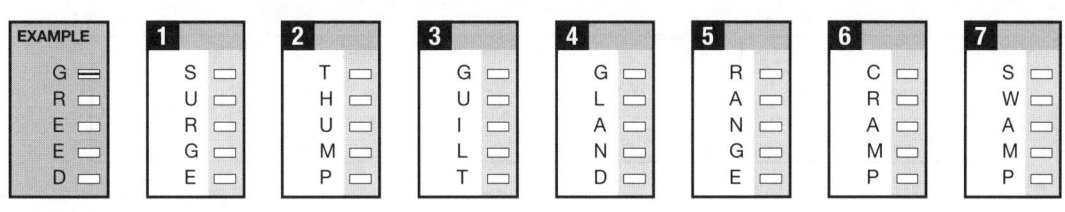

### Section 2

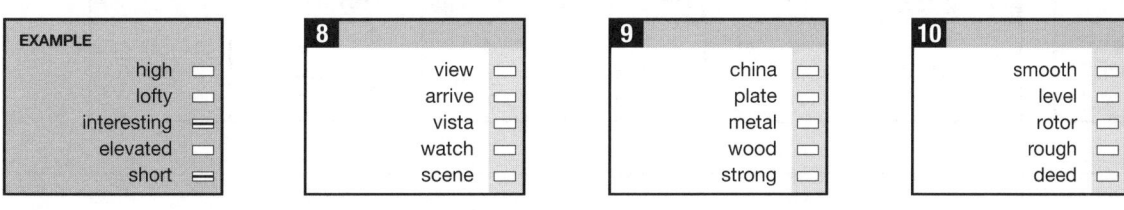

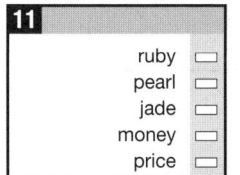 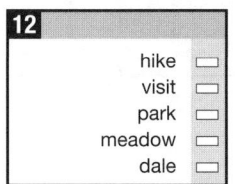 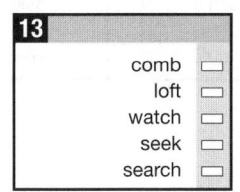 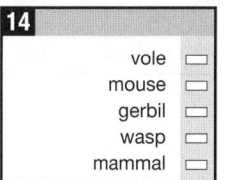

### Section 3

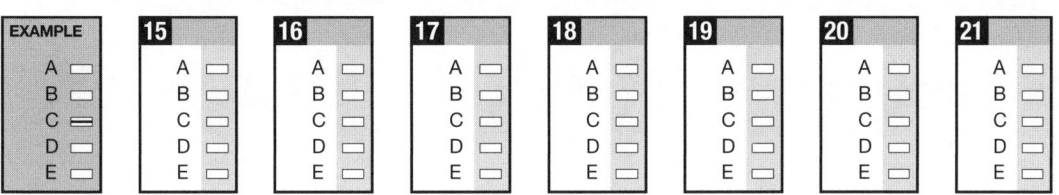

## Section 4

**22**
- Jo
- John
- Gayle
- Prabal
- Kevin

## Section 5

**EXAMPLE**
- smell
- buy
- eat
- cup
- drink
- grind

**23**
- walk
- go
- run
- bring
- brought
- take

**24**
- rapid
- destroy
- bake
- car
- dive
- engine

**25**
- courage
- calm
- weak
- hurtful
- medicine
- healed

**26**
- chair
- window
- wheel
- door
- lift
- radiator

**27**
- burn
- palm
- barracks
- pest
- pace
- ramp

**28**
- tiny
- board
- planet
- thin
- huge
- minute

**29**
- write
- discover
- stake
- struggle
- lose
- touch

## Section 6

**EXAMPLE**
- sauce
- pan
- nice
- hot
- food
- cake

**30**
- sit
- bit
- next
- one
- down
- ten

**31**
- eye
- bird
- ear
- see
- hear
- nest

**32**
- fresh
- cold
- imp
- air
- now
- lie

**33**
- wood
- rib
- gold
- bar
- den
- cage

**34**
- awe
- our
- find
- some
- loss
- time

**35**
- cask
- hob
- sea
- bled
- it
- saw

**36**
- so
- are
- err
- then
- if
- and

## Section 7

**EXAMPLE**
- The farmer
- farmer caught
- caught all ✓
- all his
- his animals

**37**
- her coat
- coat hung
- hung on
- on the
- the peg

**38**
- we should
- should wash
- wash our
- our hands
- hands properly

**39**
- he stood
- stood up
- up and
- and leaned
- leaned over

**40**
- the golfer
- golfer needed
- needed to
- to play
- play well

**41**
- they stared
- stared as
- as the
- the ogre
- ogre approached

**42**
- the beautiful
- beautiful lamb
- lamb nibbled
- nibbled fresh
- fresh grass

**43**
- she occasionally
- occasionally earns
- earns money
- money during
- during weekends

## Section 8

**44**
- A
- B
- C
- D
- E

## Section 9

**EXAMPLE**
- EAR
- TEA
- AIR ✓
- TAR
- ANT

**45**
- LOW
- ROD
- RED
- RID
- LED

**46**
- RAT
- RAW
- RAP
- RIP
- RAN

**47**
- RAP
- RIB
- RUB
- ROB
- RIP

**48**
- PAR
- SIR
- PEA
- WAR
- SEA

**49**
- RAT
- ATE
- HAT
- EAT
- AIR

**50**
- KEY
- KIT
- HIT
- HER
- EAT

**51**
- SEE
- ICE
- SEA
- TEN
- SIN

## Section 10

**EXAMPLE**
- huge =
- interesting
- quiet
- tiny
- thin
- vast =

**52**
- carcass
- cutlass
- erode
- monstrous
- corpse
- grief

**53**
- carefree
- impulsive
- loyal
- faithful
- thoughtless
- pensive

**54**
- slovenly
- intriguing
- industrious
- spectacular
- sparse
- hardworking

**55**
- direct
- remarkable
- deliberate
- discuss
- accidental
- certain

**56**
- vent
- elevator
- aisle
- duct
- shoot
- barrier

**57**
- image
- visage
- phantom
- ghost
- shadow
- scared

**58**
- follow
- mountain
- discover
- trail
- outside
- mystery

## Section 11

**EXAMPLE**
- SK
- TK =
- TP
- ST
- TV

**59**
- GH
- GJ
- JK
- KL
- KJ

**60**
- AS
- BR
- BS
- AR
- BT

**61**
- VL
- UM
- UL
- VM
- WK

**62**
- KO
- KN
- MP
- LO
- MN

**63**
- ZA
- ZY
- QR
- RS
- YX

**64**
- RI
- IR
- FS
- FT
- GR

**65**
- FM
- HO
- HN
- GM
- GO

## Section 12

**EXAMPLE**
- TILE
- HENS
- THEN =
- SING
- THIN

**66**
- REEL
- BALE
- GALE
- RAGE
- HARE

**67**
- VILE
- LEER
- LIVE
- LURE
- CLUE

**68**
- PAIR
- SCAR
- LAIR
- SPAR
- SLIP

**69**
- COVE
- DIRE
- CODE
- RIDE
- DOVE

**70**
- ROTA
- BOAT
- BARD
- DRAB
- TROD

**71**
- RUNE
- TURN
- TUNE
- HUNT
- RUNT

**72**
- TOIL
- HOWL
- WILT
- HINT
- THIN

## Section 13

| EXAMPLE | |
|---|---|
| 13 | ☐ |
| 15 | ▃ |
| 19 | ☐ |
| 22 | ☐ |
| 30 | ☐ |

**73**
- 60
- 66
- 72
- 80
- 162

**74**
- 22
- 23
- 24
- 25
- 26

**75**
- 4
- 5
- 7
- 10
- 11

**76**
- 1
- 2
- 3
- 4
- 5

**77**
- 49
- 58
- 27
- 72
- 94

**78**
- 41
- 43
- 45
- 47
- 49

**79**
- 5
- 7
- 13
- 14
- 22

## Section 14

| EXAMPLE | |
|---|---|
| MRND | ☐ |
| MNRD | ▃ |
| NMMD | ☐ |
| RMND | ☐ |
| DMNR | ☐ |

**80**
- RBQDV
- TDSFW
- UETGY
- UBTDY
- REQGV

**81**
- VOLFH
- PIFZB
- QJGAC
- UNKEG
- RKHBD

**82**
- ITHBD
- KVJDF
- KWLGJ
- MXLFH
- HSGAC

**83**
- NOISE
- LIGHT
- NIGHT
- POINT
- FAINT

**84**
- UZQIPPO
- SXOGNNM
- SZOINPM
- SZNJLRJ
- QVMELLK

**85**
- POINT
- RAISE
- WAIST
- PAINT
- PLANT

# PRACTICE PAPER 3

Student's name

School name

Date of test

## Please mark answers like this ▭

### Section 1

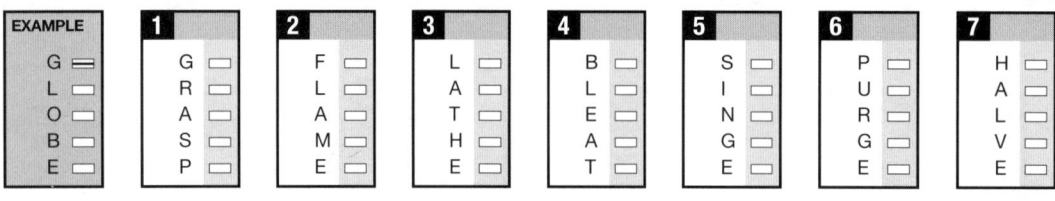

### Section 2

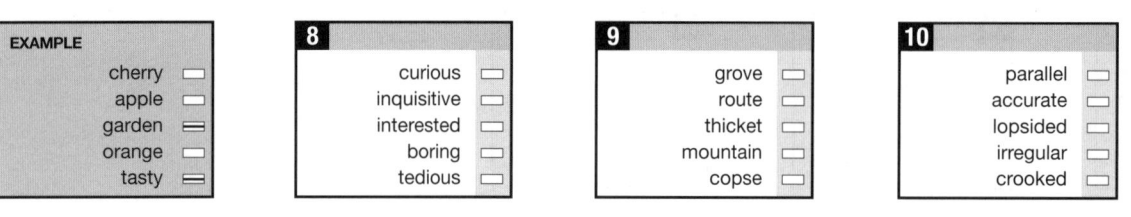

## Section 3

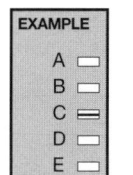  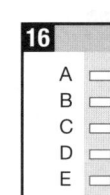 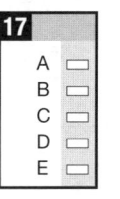 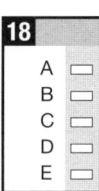 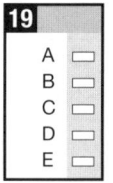 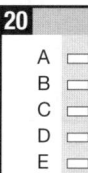 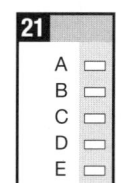

## Section 4

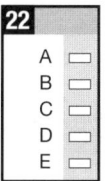

## Section 5

| EXAMPLE | | 23 | | 24 | | 25 | |
|---|---|---|---|---|---|---|---|
| eat ☐ | fly ☐ | remain ☐ | divide ☐ | care ☐ | playground ☐ | stamp ☐ | carry ☐ |
| fruit ▬ | drink ☐ | stumble ☐ | shop ☐ | hospital ☐ | understand ☐ | delivery ☐ | shopping ☐ |
| tree ☐ | meat ☐ | hotel ☐ | collect ☐ | ill ☐ | instruct ☐ | letter ☐ | plastic ☐ |

| 26 | | 27 | | 28 | | 29 | |
|---|---|---|---|---|---|---|---|
| hammer ☐ | blouse ☐ | pioneer ☐ | replace ☐ | game ☐ | shuffle ☐ | decorate ☐ | axe ☐ |
| finger ☐ | round ☐ | jungle ☐ | mechanic ☐ | roll ☐ | stack ☐ | brush ☐ | swing ☐ |
| fix ☐ | small ☐ | rocket ☐ | tools ☐ | numbers ☐ | pack ☐ | colour ☐ | woods ☐ |

## Section 6

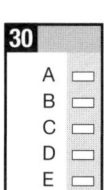

## Section 7

| EXAMPLE | | | | 31 | | | | 32 | | | | 33 | | | |
|---|---|---|---|---|---|---|---|---|---|---|---|---|---|---|---|
| light | ☐ | time | ☰ | piece | ☐ | it | ☐ | mode | ☐ | rate | ☐ | duck | ☐ | bird | ☐ |
| heavy | ☐ | house | ☰ | pill | ☐ | tee | ☐ | most | ☐ | time | ☐ | nice | ☐ | feather | ☐ |
| large | ☐ | carry | ☐ | set | ☐ | low | ☐ | long | ☐ | lea | ☐ | goose | ☐ | berry | ☐ |

| 34 | | | | 35 | | | | 36 | | | | 37 | | | |
|---|---|---|---|---|---|---|---|---|---|---|---|---|---|---|---|
| either | ☐ | or | ☐ | main | ☐ | part | ☐ | car | ☐ | pit | ☐ | ban | ☐ | den | ☐ |
| vend | ☐ | one | ☐ | old | ☐ | ace | ☐ | deep | ☐ | down | ☐ | hid | ☐ | done | ☐ |
| and | ☐ | soon | ☐ | man | ☐ | age | ☐ | new | ☐ | pet | ☐ | cord | ☐ | string | ☐ |

## Section 8

| EXAMPLE | | 38 | | 39 | | 40 | |
|---|---|---|---|---|---|---|---|
| TW | ☐ | HJ | ☐ | OP | ☐ | UX | ☐ |
| SX | ☐ | HI | ☐ | NO | ☐ | VX | ☐ |
| WX | ☰ | FH | ☐ | ON | ☐ | VY | ☐ |
| WS | ☐ | EG | ☐ | QP | ☐ | UY | ☐ |
| TZ | ☐ | FG | ☐ | NQ | ☐ | VW | ☐ |

| 41 | | 42 | | 43 | | 44 | |
|---|---|---|---|---|---|---|---|
| XV | ☐ | VP | ☐ | DG | ☐ | VU | ☐ |
| WX | ☐ | TV | ☐ | JM | ☐ | UT | ☐ |
| ZA | ☐ | VW | ☐ | MO | ☐ | IJ | ☐ |
| XY | ☐ | NP | ☐ | TQ | ☐ | LM | ☐ |
| XZ | ☐ | SU | ☐ | DZ | ☐ | ZA | ☐ |

## Section 9

| EXAMPLE | | 45 | | 46 | | 47 | |
|---|---|---|---|---|---|---|---|
| HAT | ☰ | DON | ☐ | CAT | ☐ | AYE | ☐ |
| CAT | ☐ | DID | ☐ | RUN | ☐ | ASH | ☐ |
| ATE | ☐ | TIN | ☐ | MAT | ☐ | AIL | ☐ |
| MAT | ☐ | NOD | ☐ | RAT | ☐ | ODD | ☐ |
| ANT | ☐ | DAD | ☐ | ROT | ☐ | ADD | ☐ |

| 48 | | 49 | | 50 | | 51 | |
|---|---|---|---|---|---|---|---|
| EEL | ☐ | TIN | ☐ | ERR | ☐ | WAR | ☐ |
| ALE | ☐ | OLD | ☐ | ARE | ☐ | TOT | ☐ |
| ALL | ☐ | FIX | ☐ | AIR | ☐ | CAR | ☐ |
| EVE | ☐ | OAT | ☐ | OAR | ☐ | EAT | ☐ |
| HOP | ☐ | AND | ☐ | OUR | ☐ | FAT | ☐ |

## Section 10

**EXAMPLE**
- simple
- tricky
- obvious
- strange =
- plain =
- interesting

**52**
- grave
- whole
- comical
- unsure
- graceful
- serious

**53**
- discussion
- decision
- thought
- debate
- influence
- hesitation

**54**
- imitation
- authentic
- replica
- genuine
- intricate
- peculiar

**55**
- description
- impression
- episode
- edition
- account
- revision

**56**
- poster
- diary
- booklet
- pamphlet
- reference
- design

**57**
- note
- evidence
- investigation
- solution
- thought
- proof

**58**
- robust
- brave
- thoughtless
- valiant
- vibrant
- victorious

## Section 11

**EXAMPLE**
- He hurt
- hurt his =
- his wrist
- wrist and
- and arm

**59**
- the chef
- chef happily
- happily cooked
- cooked us
- us kippers

**60**
- his wife
- wife chose
- chose sumptuous
- sumptuous new
- new carpets

**61**
- the witch
- witch opened
- opened her
- her potion
- potion book

**62**
- the super
- super hero
- hero grew
- grew even
- even stronger

**63**
- she gently
- gently bandaged
- bandaged the
- the damaged
- damaged ankle

**64**
- they did
- did not
- not swap
- swap luggage
- luggage labels

**65**
- both issues
- issues of
- of the
- the magazine
- magazine sold

## Section 12

**EXAMPLE**
- LUNG
- THUG
- HANG =
- HUNT
- HAUL

**66**
- COAT
- BANE
- BEAT
- BONE
- CONE

**67**
- LUCK
- LURK
- LIKE
- SICK
- SIRE

**68**
- PAYS
- BABY
- BAYS
- CAPS
- CABS

**69**
- PRIM
- RIPE
- MEET
- TORE
- POET

**70**
- HIPS
- SHOP
- SLIP
- HOPS
- POPS

**71**
- NAPE
- SOAP
- SNAP
- NAPS
- SPIN

**72**
- TEND
- RIDE
- BITE
- TIRE
- BIRD

## Section 13

**EXAMPLE**
- 30
- 50
- 5
- 100
- 25

**73**
- 11
- 6
- 25
- 36
- 4

**74**
- 3
- 108
- 6
- 324
- 486

**75**
- −0.1
- 2.25
- 0.25
- 2.50
- 0.45

**76**
- 9
- 116111
- 111611
- 1116111
- 116611

**77**
- 1.50
- 1.5
- 0.9
- 0.85
- 0.95

## Section 14

**EXAMPLE**
- 8
- 11
- 14
- 28
- 3

**78**
- 26
- 10
- 17
- 72
- 25

**79**
- 23
- 24
- 25
- 26
- 27

**80**
- 16
- 17
- 18
- 19
- 20

**81**
- 28
- 8
- 16
- 36
- 20

**82**
- 10
- 24
- 7
- 8
- 3

## Section 15

**83**
- 32691
- 12659
- 32659
- 14692
- 63921

**84**
- 56294
- 19462
- 15962
- 14965
- 61924

**85**
- CLOSE
- FAULT
- FEAST
- COATS
- LOCUS

# PRACTICE PAPER 4

Student's name

School name

Date of test

Please mark answers like this ▭

## Section 1

**EXAMPLE**
- lung
- heart
- human ▭
- liver
- body ▭

**1**
- screech
- beak
- scrabble
- scrape
- talon

**2**
- uncomfortable
- relaxed
- tense
- cramped
- gentle

**3**
- upbeat
- miserable
- diseased
- downbeat
- glum

**4**
- disaster
- saviour
- awesome
- cataclysm
- tragedy

**5**
- handle
- terminal
- lever
- circuit
- hilt

**6**
- conserve
- alter
- modify
- adjust
- agree

**7**
- cement
- demand
- secure
- enquire
- fuse

## Section 2

**EXAMPLE**
- A
- B
- C ▭
- D
- E

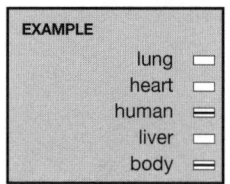
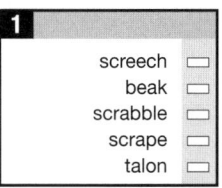
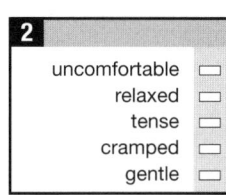
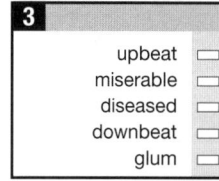

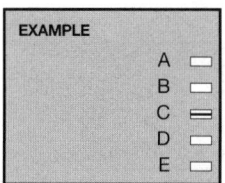
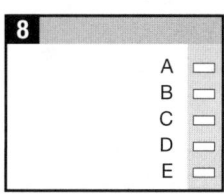

## Section 3

**13**
- A
- B
- C
- D
- E

## Section 4

EXAMPLE
- squeak
- play
- strings

- blow
- brass
- loud

**14**
- fright
- emotion
- haunted

- desire
- need
- scared

**15**
- watch
- balance
- dire

- years
- file
- live

**16**
- massive
- ice
- mountain

- water
- fire
- rocks

**17**
- arrive
- seek
- cover

- send
- dispatch
- correspond

**18**
- think
- search
- ignore

- order
- magazine
- paper

## Section 5

**19**
- A
- B
- C
- D
- E

## Section 6

EXAMPLE
- really
- born
- care

- full
- well
- free

**20**
- across
- crest
- bad

- fallen
- time
- there

**21**
- deep
- imp
- go

- down
- art
- lend

**22**
- was
- has
- have

- ten
- been
- lost

**23**
- door
- old
- candid

- ate
- place
- mouse

**24**
- van
- car
- bus

- door
- guard
- lane

## Section 7

| EXAMPLE | | 25 | | 26 | | 27 | |
|---|---|---|---|---|---|---|---|
| TU | ▬ | QO | ☐ | MP | ☐ | NG | ☐ |
| UT | ☐ | PN | ☐ | LN | ☐ | GN | ☐ |
| VS | ☐ | LJ | ☐ | LO | ☐ | NM | ☐ |
| VT | ☐ | KI | ☐ | PL | ☐ | HG | ☐ |
| US | ☐ | IQ | ☐ | IM | ☐ | HI | ☐ |

| 28 | | 29 | |
|---|---|---|---|
| HJ | ☐ | KL | ☐ |
| NM | ☐ | LN | ☐ |
| LK | ☐ | KM | ☐ |
| NK | ☐ | NO | ☐ |
| ML | ☐ | NM | ☐ |

## Section 8

| EXAMPLE | | 30 | | 31 | | 32 | |
|---|---|---|---|---|---|---|---|
| PIN | ☐ | OUT | ☐ | ARE | ☐ | ALL | ☐ |
| SIP | ☐ | ARE | ☐ | OWN | ☐ | ARE | ☐ |
| LIP | ▬ | OUR | ☐ | EEL | ☐ | AND | ☐ |
| LIE | ☐ | ANT | ☐ | ATE | ☐ | ART | ☐ |
| PIE | ☐ | ORE | ☐ | ILL | ☐ | SAT | ☐ |

| 33 | | 34 | |
|---|---|---|---|
| PAT | ☐ | MEN | ☐ |
| BAT | ☐ | MAN | ☐ |
| CAN | ☐ | TAN | ☐ |
| CAR | ☐ | TEN | ☐ |
| CAT | ☐ | OFF | ☐ |

## Section 9

| EXAMPLE | | | | 35 | | | | 36 | | | | 37 | | | |
|---|---|---|---|---|---|---|---|---|---|---|---|---|---|---|---|
| awkward | ☐ | plain | ▬ | fraction | ☐ | race | ☐ | creative | ☐ | natural | ☐ | partial | ☐ | comprehensive | ☐ |
| simple | ▬ | interesting | ☐ | attempt | ☐ | winner | ☐ | formal | ☐ | standard | ☐ | complete | ☐ | apprehensive | ☐ |
| strange | ☐ | idea | ☐ | victor | ☐ | third | ☐ | ordinary | ☐ | careful | ☐ | unfinished | ☐ | unsure | ☐ |

| 38 | | | | 39 | | | |
|---|---|---|---|---|---|---|---|
| cable | ☐ | electric | ☐ | harm | ☐ | heal | ☐ |
| string | ☐ | knot | ☐ | treat | ☐ | injure | ☐ |
| stretch | ☐ | wire | ☐ | medicine | ☐ | hospital | ☐ |

## Section 10

**EXAMPLE**
- The people
- people adored
- adored dancing
- dancing and
- and singing

**40**
- the bee
- bee hive
- hive started
- started to
- to vibrate

**41**
- the skate
- skate rink
- rink now
- now opens
- opens daily

**42**
- the pale
- pale aqua
- aqua yacht
- yacht sailed
- sailed away

**43**
- our young
- young librarian
- librarian is
- is really
- really helpful

**44**
- they listened
- listened as
- as the
- the teacher
- teacher explained

## Section 11

**EXAMPLE**
- WAD
- SIP
- PAD
- SAD
- SID

**45**
- DEW
- DYE
- WAY
- YEW
- YAW

**46**
- NIL
- SLY
- KIN
- LIE
- SIN

**47**
- SPAN
- SCAN
- PACY
- CAPS
- CUSP

**48**
- FLAN
- SHIP
- CASH
- CHIN
- SHIN

**49**
- MATE
- MANE
- TUNE
- HEAT
- HATE

**50**
- PART
- PANT
- CART
- LAST
- CATS

**51**
- VINE
- LIVE
- VENT
- SENT
- VILE

## Section 12

**EXAMPLE**
- 20
- 26
- 22
- 40
- 32

**52**
- 63
- 56
- 72
- 49
- 70

**53**
- 4.921
- 4.93
- 5.93
- 5.921
- 4.9201

**54**
- 14
- 15
- 16
- 17
- 18

**55**
- 3
- 4
- 5
- 6
- 7

**56**
- 70
- 75
- 82
- 91
- 102

**57**
- 8
- 9
- 10
- 11
- 12

## Section 13

**EXAMPLE**
- 15
- 22
- 20
- 30
- 28

**58**
- 63
- 8
- 16
- 81
- 18

**59**
- 64
- 40
- 20
- 4
- 68

**60**
- 16
- 15
- 56
- 57
- 31

**61**
- 35
- 21
- 28
- 98
- 7

**62**
- 15
- 60
- 8
- 13
- 30

## Section 14

**63**
- 67825
- 61295
- 61975
- 25197
- 21597

**64**
- 29781
- 52891
- 58291
- 59271
- 72581

**65**
- PILES
- PAILS
- PELTS
- PLATE
- SPITE

## Section 15

**66**
- GAPES
- PARTS
- GRATE
- GRAPE
- GALES

**67**
- SPARE
- SLATE
- STRAP
- PASTE
- PAGES

**68**
- 56137
- 46837
- 45273
- 48137
- 48957

## Section 16

**EXAMPLE**
- above
- near
- around
- close
- below
- over

**69**
- expensive
- expand
- experience
- contract
- dear
- constant

**70**
- vigour
- nimble
- dexterity
- energy
- skill
- lethargy

**71**
- difficult
- genuine
- ruthless
- merciful
- confused
- catastrophic

**72**
- interrogate
- deviate
- aggravate
- intensify
- soothe
- demand

**73**
- eliminate
- luminous
- elevate
- disqualify
- dark
- hoist

## Section 17

**EXAMPLE**
- seen
- green
- lean ▦
- clean
- open

**74**
- gave
- rave
- rage
- gear
- ever

**75**
- vine
- dine
- dive
- vein
- vain

**76**
- dive
- dire
- dirt
- ride
- tire

**77**
- cats
- cans
- hats
- chat
- cast

**78**
- sew
- toe
- sow
- tor
- wet

## Section 18

**EXAMPLE**
- MG
- OF ▦
- LH
- KE
- GN

**79**
- LQ
- LP
- MR
- KP
- JO

**80**
- ZY
- AX
- AY
- BZ
- YZ

**81**
- SJ
- WK
- WS
- SY
- RJ

**82**
- JF
- JG
- JE
- KF
- KG

**83**
- KJ
- KI
- MK
- ML
- JI

**84**
- IC
- IE
- HD
- HC
- BD

**85**
- OY
- PZ
- QX
- PX
- QY

# PRACTISE & PASS 11+

# VERBAL REASONING
## ANSWERS AND ADVICE FOR PARENTS

Read this <u>before</u> the student starts taking any of the practice test papers.

## Contents

| | |
|---|---|
| ⚙ Timings and rules for Verbal Reasoning practice papers | 2 |
| ⚙ Suggested mock test schedule | 2 |
| ⚙ Marking the tests: correct answers and answer explanations | 4 |
|     Practice paper 1 | 4 |
|     Practice paper 2 | 10 |
|     Practice paper 3 | 16 |
|     Practice paper 4 | 21 |
| ⚙ How to improve scores | 29 |

---

© Peter Williams and Trotman Publishing, 2015

The right of Peter Williams to be identified as the author of this work has been asserted by him in accordance with the Copyright, Designs and Patents Act, 1988.

All rights reserved. No part of this publication may be transmitted in any form or by any means, or stored in a retrieval system without prior written permission from the publisher.

First published 2015 by Trotman Publishing, a division of Crimson Publishing Ltd, 19–21c Charles Street, Bath BA1 1HX.

ISBN 978 1 84455 430 0

A catalogue record for this book is available from the British Library.

# TIMINGS AND RULES FOR VERBAL REASONING PRACTICE PAPERS

### SETTING THE TEST

- Students should be allowed 50 minutes to complete each verbal reasoning paper.
- Do not read any examples to the student.
- Students are expected to read all instructions and examples themselves within the 50 minutes.
- All final answers should be marked on the multiple choice answer grid. No further working should appear on this grid.
- Time the test precisely and stop the student when the allotted time is over.
- Students may be informed when they are halfway through the allotted time and when there are five minutes remaining.

### GUIDANCE FOR TESTING

- Do explain to students before the test that there will be some very difficult questions and they could appear at any point in the test. Tell students to mark these on the paper and come back to them. Tell them not to waste time fretting about really tough questions, just to get on and answer those questions they know how to!
- Get students to check they have marked an answer in each answer grid – often students forget to do this for each question or mark them in the wrong order or even mark two on one grid and none on the next.

## SUGGESTED MOCK TEST SCHEDULE

If you want the student to take the practice papers in a mock test format, then you can follow the suggestions below on how to do this. All exams are different in nature so the order in which papers are given and which question styles are included can vary. If the student has worked through *Practise & Pass 11+ Level One: Discover Verbal Reasoning* and *Practise & Pass 11+ Level Two: Develop Verbal Reasoning* they will be familiar with the most common question styles.

### SET UP

- Set up a clear desk. Have a pencil, rubber and spare blank paper set out.
- Make sure a simple, analogue clock is easily visible.
- Follow all rules and timings precisely (see above).
- Do not give any extra help even if you can see that the student is making a mistake.
- If the student requires a bathroom break during a paper, let them but explain that no extra time will be given.
- Try to get the student to use the full amount of time – they will not be allowed to leave the room early in the actual exam.

**INCLUDING OTHER TESTS**

If you want to replicate a true exam experience, give the student other test types to do, using the other titles in the *Practise & Pass 11+ Level Three* series. Follow the suggested times given for each type of test and give the student a 10 minute break to have a quick drink and use the bathroom after completing each test.

**Note:** It is rare for students to have to take papers in all areas so it is important for parents to find out which papers are relevant and have the student take only those.

Once you know which papers your child needs to sit then set out a schedule as follows.

- Test 1 – 50 minutes
- Break – 10 minutes
- Test 2 – 50 minutes
- Break – 10 minutes
- Test 3 – 50 minutes

Please note that non-verbal reasoning has different timings to English, maths and verbal reasoning so take account of this when planning your 'mock' day for your child.

**WRITING PAPER**

If you want to set the writing paper as part of your mock English test choose just one title for your child to do. Do not give them a choice of titles unless the school for which you are preparing specifically does this. If you decide to give your child more than one set of mock exams, try choosing a different type of writing title so that they have experience of creative writing and non-fiction styles.

**Note:** Different schools allocate different time limits for the writing paper (if they are setting one), from 20 minutes to 45 minutes. You should check with the school how much time will be allowed but if no time is given, or you are unable to find out, allow the student 30 minutes to sit the writing paper.

# MARKING THE TESTS: CORRECT ANSWERS AND ANSWER EXPLANATIONS

The following pages contain the correct answers for papers 1, 2, 3 and 4. If a student has answered incorrectly go through the question with them to ensure they understand where they went wrong. If they are still struggling go back to the relevant sections of *Practise & Pass 11+ Level One: Discover Verbal Reasoning* and *Practise & Pass 11+ Level Two: Develop Verbal Reasoning* and practise those types of question again. You can also refer to the section on how to improve scores (page 29) for tips on further practice.

When marking the papers remember there are no half marks – the answer should be marked as either correct or incorrect. Any workings out on scrap paper should not be marked. If the student has written the correct answer on a piece of working out paper but marked the incorrect letter on the corresponding grid answer sheet, the answer is incorrect.

It is vital that students practise how to mark the correct answer on the multiple choice grids so do not consider any working out on scrap paper.

## PRACTICE PAPER 1

### Section 1

| Question | Answer | Explanation |
|---|---|---|
| 1. | E | to make GLAD and HEART |
| 2. | B | to make RING and PLUMB |
| 3. | T | to make ISLE and PAINT |
| 4. | C | to make ARID and WINCED |
| 5. | F | to make RATS and BELIEFS |
| 6. | D | to make PENS and WINDS |
| 7. | N | to make BRIG and CHOSEN |

### Section 2

| Question | Answer | Explanation |
|---|---|---|
| 8. | E | Using the code given the sum is $2 + 6 = 8$, $8 \times 3 = 24$, then divide by $4 = 6$. |
| 9. | A | Using the code given the sum is $58 - (7 \times 8) = 58 - 56 = 2$. |
| 10. | B | Using the code given the sum is $20 - 8 - 7 = 5$. |
| 11. | E | Using the code given the sum is $(7 \times 9) = 63 - (4 \times 6) = 24$, so $63 - 24 = 39$ and $- 6 \times 5 = 30$ so $39 - 30 = 9$. |
| 12. | A | Using the code given the sum is $4 \times 7 = 28 - 25 = 3$. |
| 13. | B | Using the code given the sum is $144 - (11 \times 12) = 144 - 132 = 12$. |

## Section 3

| Question | Answer | Explanation |
|---|---|---|
| 14. | Tracey | Tracey buys rice, potatoes, cheese and milk (4 items). |

## Section 4

| Question | Answer | Explanation |
|---|---|---|
| 15. | pink note | knot |
| 16. | stifle every | flee |
| 17. | was lower | slow |
| 18. | if our | four |
| 19. | thumb endured | bend |
| 20. | reef ended | fend |
| 21. | general ambience | lamb |

## Section 5

| Question | Answer | Explanation |
|---|---|---|
| 22. | run, bung | flow means run; block means bung |
| 23. | toil, determine | struggle means toil; decide means determine |
| 24. | fear, tranquil | fret means fear; tranquil means calm |
| 25. | emotion, sense | anger is an emotion; taste is a sense |
| 26. | train, light | Remove the first letter of each word to find the correct word in the group. |
| 27. | space, ocean | a rocket is used in space; a submarine is used in an ocean |
| 28. | colleague, foe | friend means colleague; enemy means foe |

## Section 6

| Question | Answer | Explanation |
|---|---|---|
| 29. | traverse, cross | traverse and cross are synonyms |
| 30. | anguish, worry | anguish and worry are synonyms |
| 31. | diligent, meticulous | diligent and meticulous are synonyms |
| 32. | creative, imaginative | creative and imaginative are synonyms |
| 33. | drowse, snooze | drowse and snooze are synonyms |
| 34. | margin, border | margin and border are synonyms |
| 35. | scrape, rasp | scrape and rasp are synonyms |

## Section 7

| Question | Answer | Explanation |
|---|---|---|
| 36. | begin, attempt | The other words mean 'to end'. |
| 37. | musical, dancing | The other words are musical instruments. |
| 38. | pause, proper | The other words are punctuation marks. |
| 39. | expensive, silver | The other words are items of jewellery. |
| 40. | foundation, domain | The other words are types of dwelling. |
| 41. | explain, deliver | The other words describe something funny. |
| 42. | extreme, special | The other words all mean ordinary. |

## Section 8

| Question | Answer | Explanation |
|---|---|---|
| 43. | LET | to make TABLETS |
| 44. | ONE | to make STATIONERY |
| 45. | RUT | to make TRUTH |
| 46. | EVE | to make SEVERAL |
| 47. | OWN | to make DOWNLOADED |
| 48. | TAP | to make STAPLED |
| 49. | VAN | to make ADVANCE |

## Section 9

| Question | Answer | Explanation |
|---|---|---|
| 50. | E | Vera sometimes catches the same bus as Jeffrey. |

## Section 10

| Question | Answer | Explanation |
|---|---|---|
| 51. | CB | Each letter goes back one each time. |
| 52. | ZV | The first letter goes back two each time and the second letter goes forward two each time. |
| 53. | ZR | The first letter repeats twice then goes forward three; the second letter goes back two then forward five. |
| 54. | FF | The first letter goes forward two each time; the second letter goes forward one for the next sequence, then back four for the sequence after that, then forward one again and so on. |
| 55. | GA | The first letter goes back two each time; the second letter goes back three each time. |
| 56. | IK | The first letter goes forward one each time; the second letter goes two places past the previous letter alternating forwards then back – draw these on the alphabet to see. |
| 57. | MN | Each letter goes two places past the previous letter alternating forwards then back – draw these on the alphabet to see. |

## Section 11

| Question | Answer | Explanation |
|---|---|---|
| 58. | bar, row | barrow |
| 59. | ran, sack | ransack |
| 60. | pad, lock | padlock |
| 61. | par, don | pardon |
| 62. | for, age | forage |
| 63. | pit, fall | pitfall |
| 64. | cob, bled | cobbled |

## Section 12

| Question | Answer | Explanation |
| --- | --- | --- |
| 65. | WIND | The missing word is created using the last two letters of the first word (ND) and first two letters of the second word (WI) and then reversing the order to get WIND. |
| 66. | TORN | The missing word uses the first and fourth letters of the first word (TN) and letters two and three of the second word (OR) and changing order to create TORN. |
| 67. | SNIP | The missing word uses letters one and three (SN) of the first word and letters two and four (IP) of the second word to create SNIP. |
| 68. | LUNG | The missing word uses letters two and four (LG) of the first word and letters two and three (UN) of the second word and amends the order to create LUNG. |
| 69. | SHOW | The missing word uses letters three and four (SH) of the first word and letters one and two (WO) of the second word and amends the order to create SHOW. |
| 70. | RIPE | The missing word uses letters one and two (PE) of the first word and letters three and four (IR) of the second word and amends the order to create RIPE. |
| 71. | LONE | The missing word uses letters two and three (NO) of the first word and letters one and two (LE) of the second word and amends the order to create LONE. |

## Section 13

| Question | Answer | Explanation |
| --- | --- | --- |
| 72. | 10 | The amount subtracted each time starts at 6 then 4, then 2 and then starts to increase by the same amount so subtract 4, then 6 e.g.: $-6, -4, -2, -4, -6$. |
| 73. | 67 | The pattern goes +2, +4, +8, +16 then + 32 to get 67. |
| 74. | 19 | This question contains alternate sequences increasing by 5 each time. |
| 75. | 22 | This question contains alternate patterns, the first goes down by one each time, the other increases by four each time. |
| 76. | 7 | This sequence adds four, subtracts one, adds four, subtracts one and so on. |
| 77. | 29 | This sequence adds the two previous numbers to make the next number in the sequence. |
| 78. | 16 | This sequence is an alternate pattern that doubles the numbers each time. |

## Section 14

| Question | Answer | Explanation |
| --- | --- | --- |
| 79. | IR | The first letter goes forward three while the second letter goes back three. |
| 80. | RT | The first letter goes forward three while the second letter goes forward seven. |
| 81. | ZY | Each letter goes back three. |
| 82. | DE | The first letter goes forward one while the second letter goes back one. |
| 83. | PS | The first letter goes back one while the second letter goes forward one. |
| 84. | BY | Each letter goes back five. |
| 85. | DF | The first letter goes back one while the second letter goes forward three. |

# PRACTICE PAPER 2

## Section 1

| Question | Answer | Explanation |
|---|---|---|
| 1. | G | to make SURE and GRIDS |
| 2. | T | to make HUMP and STALE |
| 3. | U | to make GILT and AUNT |
| 4. | N | to make GLAD and SLUNG |
| 5. | N | to make RAGE and RINSE |
| 6. | C | to make RAMP and PITCH |
| 7. | P | to make SWAM and STAPLE |

## Section 2

| Question | Answer | Explanation |
|---|---|---|
| 8. | arrive, watch | The others are types of view. |
| 9. | plate, strong | The others are types of material. |
| 10. | smooth, rough | The others are palindromes (spelt the same way backwards and forwards). |
| 11. | money, price | The others are precious stones. |
| 12. | hike, visit | The others are types of field. |
| 13. | loft, watch | The others mean to look for something. |
| 14. | wasp, mammal | The others are small rodents. |

## Section 3

| Question | Answer | Explanation |
|---|---|---|
| 15. | D | Using the code given the calculation is $4 + 12 = 16$, then $\times 2 = 32$, then divide by $4 = 8$. |
| 16. | B | Using the code given the calculation is $6 \times 8 = 48$ and $3 \times 4 = 12$. $48 \div 12 = 4$. |
| 17. | C | Using the code given the calculation is $24 \div 8 = 3$, then $+ (2 \times 3) = 3 + 6 = 9$. |
| 18. | C | Using the code given the calculation is $15 + 6 = 21$, then $\times 3 = 63$, then $\div 9 = 7$. |
| 19. | C | Using the code given the calculation is $3 \times 4 = 12$, then $\times 5 = 60$, then $\div 12 = 5$. |
| 20. | E | Using the code given the calculation is $14 \times 12 = 168 - (11 \times 13) = 143$ so $168 - 143 = 25$. |
| 21. | C | Using the code given the calculation is $12 \times 25 = 300$, then $\div 20 = 15$. |

## Section 4

| Question | Answer | Explanation |
| --- | --- | --- |
| 22. | John | John sits in the middle of the row as the order is Prabal, Kevin, John, Jo and Gayle. Note: the order could be reversed but does not change the answer. |

## Section 5

| Question | Answer | Explanation |
| --- | --- | --- |
| 23. | go, take | go is the present tense of went and take is the present tense of took |
| 24. | bake, dive | remove the second letter from each word |
| 25. | weak, hurtful | weak means feeble and hurtful means painful |
| 26. | wheel, lift | a wheel rotates and a lift elevates |
| 27. | barracks, pace | camp means barracks and step means pace |
| 28. | tiny, huge | vast is the opposite of tiny and minuscule is the opposite of huge |
| 29. | stake, struggle | claim means stake and flail means struggle |

## Section 6

| Question | Answer | Explanation |
| --- | --- | --- |
| 30. | bit, ten | bitten |
| 31. | ear, nest | earnest |
| 32. | imp, air | impair |
| 33. | rib, cage | ribcage |
| 34. | awe, some | awesome |
| 35. | hob, bled | hobbled |
| 36. | err, and | errand |

## Section 7

| Question | Answer | Explanation |
|---|---|---|
| 37. | coat hung | oath |
| 38. | wash our | hour |
| 39. | leaned over | dove |
| 40. | golfer needed | fern |
| 41. | ogre approached | reap |
| 42. | beautiful lamb | full |
| 43. | occasionally earns | year |

## Section 8

| Question | Answer | Explanation |
|---|---|---|
| 44. | D | As Bruce needs to score above 80% to pass only this statement must be true – Bruce did not pass the driving test. |

## Section 9

| Question | Answer | Explanation |
|---|---|---|
| 45. | RED | to make INGREDIENTS |
| 46. | RAP | to make AUTOGRAPHS |
| 47. | ROB | to make ACROBAT |
| 48. | SEA | to make SEARCHED |
| 49. | RAT | to make DECORATED |
| 50. | HIT | to make ARCHITECT |
| 51. | ICE | to make MAGNIFICENT |

## Section 10

| Question | Answer | Explanation |
| --- | --- | --- |
| 52. | carcass, corpse | carcass and corpse are synonyms |
| 53. | loyal, faithful | loyal and faithful are synonyms |
| 54. | industrious, hardworking | industrious and hardworking are synonyms |
| 55. | deliberate, discuss | deliberate and discuss are synonyms |
| 56. | vent, duct | vent and duct are synonyms |
| 57. | phantom, ghost | phantom and ghost are synonyms |
| 58. | follow, trail | follow and trail are synonyms |

## Section 11

| Question | Answer | Explanation |
| --- | --- | --- |
| 59. | KL | Each letter goes forward three for the first sequence and then back one for the next sequence and so on. |
| 60. | AS | The first letter goes back one for the first sequence, then two, then three and so on. The second letter goes forward one for the first sequence, then two, then three and so on. |
| 61. | UL | The first letter goes forward by five for the first sequence, then four, then three and so on. The second letter goes back by two each time. |
| 62. | LO | The first letter goes forward by two each time; the second letter goes back by two each time. |
| 63. | ZY | This question uses alternate patterns that skip a set of letters each time so there are two patterns happening in this question. CB, BA and AZ form the first set and MN, NO and OP form the second. The first letter of the first pair goes back by one, then the first letter of the next pair goes forward by one. The second letters follow the same pattern. |
| 64. | GR | The first letter goes back by one each time; the second letter goes forward by one each time. |
| 65. | FM | The letters both go back by three for the first sequence and then back by one for the second sequence and so on. |

## Section 12

| Question | Answer | Explanation |
|---|---|---|
| 66. | BALE | The missing word uses letters three and four (AB) of the first word and letters three and four (EL) of the second word and amends the order to create BALE. |
| 67. | LURE | The missing word uses letters two and three (UR) of the first word and letters one and four (EL) of the second word and amends the order to create LURE. |
| 68. | SCAR | The missing word uses letters one and three (CA) from the first word and letters three and four (RS) from the second word and amends the order to create SCAR. |
| 69. | DOVE | The missing word uses letters two and four (OE) from the first word and letters one and three (DV) from the second word and amends the order to create DOVE. |
| 70. | ROTA | The missing word uses letters two and four (AT) from the first word and letters two and four (OR) from the second word and amends the order to create ROTA. |
| 71. | TUNE | The missing word uses letters one and two (EN) from the first word and letters two and four (UT) from the second word and amends the order to create TUNE. |
| 72. | HOWL | The missing word uses letters one and four (WH) from the first word and letters one and three (LO) from the second word and amends the order to create HOWL. |

## Section 13

| Question | Answer | Explanation |
|---|---|---|
| 73. | 162 | In this question the numbers are multiplied by three each time. |
| 74. | 25 | This question uses alternate patterns; the first goes down by five each time and the second goes up by four each time, so 37 goes to 32 then to 27 and 17 goes to 21 then 25. |
| 75. | 4 | This is an alternating pattern. The larger numbers are reduced by the size of the number which follows them each time. The smaller numbers increase by one each time. So 19 − 2 = 17 − 3 = 14 and the next number will be 4. |
| 76. | 2 | In this question the numbers are halved each time. |
| 77. | 58 | This question uses alternate patterns but both add 22 each time. |
| 78. | 47 | The sequence in this question adds the two previous numbers to make the next. |
| 79. | 14 | This question uses alternate patterns; the first goes up one each time and second goes up five. |

## Section 14

| Question | Answer | Explanation |
| --- | --- | --- |
| 80. | UETGY | Each letter goes forward two to make the code letter, so S is U, C is E, R is T, E is G and W is Y. |
| 81. | PIFZB | Each letter goes back three to make the code letter, so S is P, L is I, I is F, C is Z and E is B. |
| 82. | KWLGJ | Each letter goes forward by one then by two then by three and so on to make the code letter, so J is K, U is W, I is L, C is G and E is J. |
| 83. | NIGHT | Each letter goes forward by one to make the code letter so go backwards by one each time to make the new word. So O is N, J is I, H is G, I is H and U is T. |
| 84. | SZNJLRJ | The letters go back by one then forward by one, back by two then forward by two and so on to make the code letters, so T is S, Y is Z, P is N, H is J, the first O is L, the second O is R and N is J. |
| 85. | PAINT | Each letter goes forward by two to make the code letters, so R is P, C is A, K is I, P is N and V is T as we have to go back two each time to make the word. |

# PRACTICE PAPER 3

## Section 1

| Question | Answer | Explanation |
|---|---|---|
| 1. | R | to make GASP and GRAPE |
| 2. | F | to make LAME and STIFLE |
| 3. | H | to make LATE and SHORT |
| 4. | L | to make BEAT and GRAVEL |
| 5. | E | to make SING and SPEAR or SPARE |
| 6. | P | to make URGE and CRAMP |
| 7. | V | to make HALE and VALVE |

## Section 2

| Question | Answer | Explanation |
|---|---|---|
| 8. | boring, tedious | The others mean the opposite of boring and tedious. |
| 9. | route, mountain | The others are descriptions of parts of woods. |
| 10. | parallel, accurate | The others mean inaccurate. |
| 11. | capture, deluge | The others mean to evade. |
| 12. | dull, cracked | The others mean the surfaces have been made shiny. |
| 13. | petulant, practice | The others mean to have some amount of knowledge. |
| 14. | rainforest, warm | The others mean up to date. |

## Section 3

| Question | Answer | Explanation |
|---|---|---|
| 15. | E – See Further practice on p.33 | Using the code given the sum is $3 \times 9 = 27$ and $5 \times 7 = 35$, then $27 + 35 = 62$. |
| 16. | C | Using the code given the sum is $4 + 6 + 8 = 18$ and $2 + 10 = 12$, then $18 - 12 = 6$. |
| 17. | E – See Further practice on p.33 | Using the code given the sum is $5 \times 7 = 35$ and $2 \times 10 = 20$, then $35 - 20 = 15$. |
| 18. | D – See Further practice on p.33 | Using the code given the sum is $7 \times 8 = 56$ and $5 \times 9 = 45$, then $56 - 45 - 2 = 9$. |
| 19. | A | Using the code given the sum is $2 + 10 = 12$, then $\times 7 = 84$ and $17 + 25 = 42$, then $84 \div 42 = 2$. |
| 20. | A | Using the code given the sum is $14 \times 50 = 700$ and $12 + 13 = 25$, then $700 \div 25 = 28$. |
| 21. | B | Using the code given the sum is $6 + 9 = 15$, then $\div 5 = 3$. |

### Section 4

| Question | Answer | Explanation |
|---|---|---|
| 22. | B | Eric wears orange shorts and a blue scarf. |

### Section 5

| Question | Answer | Explanation |
|---|---|---|
| 23. | stumble, collect | trip means stumble and gather means collect |
| 24. | care, instruct | a nurse cares for people and a teacher instructs them |
| 25. | letter, shopping | a letter goes in an envelope and shopping goes in a bag |
| 26. | finger, blouse | a nail is part of a finger and a button is part of a blouse |
| 27. | pioneer, mechanic | a pioneer explores and a mechanic repairs |
| 28. | roll, shuffle | dice are rolled and cards are shuffled |
| 29. | brush, axe | a brush is used to paint and an axe is used to chop |

### Section 6

| Question | Answer | Explanation |
|---|---|---|
| 30. | D | Lola is 6, Edward is 18, Craig is 13 and Wendola is 15, so Edward is older than Wendola. |

### Section 7

| Question | Answer | Explanation |
|---|---|---|
| 31. | set, tee | settee |
| 32. | mode, rate | moderate |
| 33. | goose, berry | gooseberry |
| 34. | vend, or | vendor |
| 35. | man, age | manage |
| 36. | car, pet | carpet |
| 37. | hid, den | hidden |

## Section 8

| Question | Answer | Explanation |
|---|---|---|
| 38. | FH | Each letter goes back by one. |
| 39. | OP | The first letter goes forward by two and the second letter goes forward by four. |
| 40. | UY | The first letter goes forward by one and the second letter goes forward by two. |
| 41. | XZ | The first letter goes back by one and the second letter goes forward by three. |
| 42. | VP | The first letter goes forward by four and the second letter goes back by four. |
| 43. | TQ | The letters 'mirror' each other based on where they appear in the alphabet (imagine folding the alphabet in half). |
| 44. | ZA | Both letters go back by six. |

## Section 9

| Question | Answer | Explanation |
|---|---|---|
| 45. | DID | to make CANDIDATES |
| 46. | RAT | to make MARATHON |
| 47. | ADD | to make WADDLED |
| 48. | ALL | to make REALLY |
| 49. | OLD | to make FOLDING |
| 50. | OUR | to make ARMOUR |
| 51. | WAR | to make WARILY |

## Section 10

| Question | Answer | Explanation |
|---|---|---|
| 52. | grave, serious | grave and serious are synonyms |
| 53. | discussion, debate | discussion and debate are synonyms |
| 54. | authentic, genuine | authentic and genuine are synonyms |
| 55. | description, account | description and account are synonyms |
| 56. | booklet, pamphlet | booklet and pamphlet are synonyms |
| 57. | evidence, proof | evidence and proof are synonyms |
| 58. | brave, valiant | brave and valiant are synonyms |

## Section 11

| Question | Answer | Explanation |
|---|---|---|
| 59. | us kippers | skip |
| 60. | wife chose | echo |
| 61. | witch opened | chop or hope |
| 62. | hero grew | ogre |
| 63. | damaged ankle | dank |
| 64. | swap luggage | plug |
| 65. | both issues | this or hiss |

## Section 12

| Question | Answer | Explanation |
|---|---|---|
| 66. | BONE | The missing word uses letters one and two (BO) of the first word and letters three and four (NE) of the second word to create BONE. |
| 67. | LURK | The missing word uses letters one and four (LK) of the first word and letters two and three (UR) of the second word and amends the order to create LURK. |
| 68. | BABY | The missing word uses letters two and four (AY) of the first word and letters one and three of the second word (BB) and amends the order to create BABY. |
| 69. | PRIM | The missing word uses letters one and three (RP) of the first word and letters two and three (MI) of the second word and amends the order to create PRIM. |
| 70. | HOPS | The missing word uses letters one and two (SH) of the first word and letters one and three (PO) of the second word and amends the order to create HOPS. |
| 71. | NAPE | The missing word uses letters two and three (AN) of the first word and letters three and four (PE) of the second and amends the order to create NAPE. |
| 72. | BIRD | The missing word uses letters one and four (BD) of the first word and letters two and three (RI) of the second word and amends the order to create BIRD. |

### Section 13

| Question | Answer | Explanation |
|---|---|---|
| 73. | 25 | This question uses alternate sequences; the first sequence goes down by four each time and the second sequence goes up by four each time. |
| 74. | 486 | This question multiplies each number by three each time. |
| 75. | 2.25 | This question halves each number each time. |
| 76. | 111611 | The sequence in this question adds the number 1 to the front of the number and then adds the number 1 to the end of the number. |
| 77. | 0.9 | This question adds 0.15 each time. |

### Section 14

| Question | Answer | Explanation |
|---|---|---|
| 78. | 25 | To find the relationship you double the number on the left of the brackets then add the number on the right. |
| 79. | 25 | To find the relationship you multiply the numbers outside the brackets then add one. |
| 80. | 16 | To find the relationship you add the numbers outside the brackets then halve the total. |
| 81. | 16 | To find the relationship you divide the number on the right of the brackets by the number on the left, then double the total. |
| 82. | 8 | To find the relationship you add the numbers outside the brackets then divide the total by three. |

### Section 15

| Question | Answer | Explanation |
|---|---|---|
| 83. | 12659 | The key to this code is the digit 2 which appears in all three codes in three different places. There is only one letter it can be – 'o'. Using this we can see that 37269 = float, 32185 = focus and 16427 = carol. We can work out the other answers from this information. So COAST = 12659. |
| 84. | 61924 | Using the same code as above (37269 = float, 32185 = focus and 16427 = carol) we can see that A = 6, C = 1, T = 9, O = 2 and R = 4. |
| 85. | FAULT | Using the same code above (37269 = float, 32185 = focus and 16427 = carol) we need to find the letter that each number relates to. Using the code we can see that 3 = F, 6 = A, 8 = U, 7 = L and 9 = T so the word is FAULT. |

# PRACTICE PAPER 4

## Section 1

| Question | Answer | Explanation |
|---|---|---|
| 1. | beak, talon | the others are verbs |
| 2. | relaxed, gentle | the others have the opposite meaning |
| 3. | upbeat, diseased | the others mean unhappy |
| 4. | saviour, awesome | the others mean some terrible event |
| 5. | terminal, circuit | the others mean something which is held |
| 6. | conserve, agree | the others mean to change things in some way |
| 7. | demand, enquire | the others mean to fix something to one place |

## Section 2

| Question | Answer | Explanation |
|---|---|---|
| 8. | E | Using the code given the sum is $3 \times 9 = 27$, then $- 5 = 22$, then $+ 7 = 29$. |
| 9. | D | Using the code given the sum is $10 \div 4 = 2.5$, then $\times 8 = 20$. |
| 10. | C | Using the code given the sum is $10 + 15 = 25$, then $\div 5 = 5$, then $+ 2 = 7$. |
| 11. | B | Using the code given the sum is $5 - 7 = -2$, then $+ 16 (2 \times 8) = 14$, then $- 9 = 5$. |
| 12. | B | Using the code given the sum is $25 - 16 = 9$, then $\times 4 = 36$, then $\div 9 (18 \div 2) = 4$. |

## Section 3

| Question | Answer | Explanation |
|---|---|---|
| 13. | B | Rick only went on the Ghost Train. |

## Section 4

| Question | Answer | Explanation |
|---|---|---|
| 14. | fright, desire | fear means fright and envy means desire |
| 15. | dire, file | dire is made from ride and file is made from life |
| 16. | ice, water | a glacier is made from ice and a geyser from water |
| 17. | arrive, dispatch | arrive is what happens after embarking and deliver is what happens after dispatching |
| 18. | search, order | search means browse and order means catalogue |

## Section 5

| Question | Answer | Explanation |
|---|---|---|
| 19. | D | Matt goes to four classes. |

## Section 6

| Question | Answer | Explanation |
|---|---|---|
| 20. | crest, fallen | crestfallen |
| 21. | imp, art | impart |
| 22. | has, ten | hasten |
| 23. | candid, ate | candidate |
| 24. | van, guard | vanguard |

## Section 7

| Question | Answer | Explanation |
|---|---|---|
| 25. | KI | Each letter goes back three. |
| 26. | LO | Each letter goes forward seven. |
| 27. | NG | The first letter goes forward three and the second letter goes back three. |
| 28. | ML | The first letter goes back six and the second letter goes back five. |
| 29. | KM | The first letter goes back 10 places and the second letter goes back five places. |

## Section 8

| Question | Answer | Explanation |
|---|---|---|
| 30. | OUR | to make DEVOURED |
| 31. | OWN | to make DOWNPOUR |
| 32. | ALL | to make FINALLY |
| 33. | CAT | to make DELICATE |
| 34. | MAN | to make PERFORMANCE |

## Section 9

| Question | Answer | Explanation |
|---|---|---|
| 35. | victor, winner | victor and winner are synonyms |
| 36. | ordinary, standard | ordinary and standard are synonyms |
| 37. | complete, comprehensive | complete and comprehensive are synonyms |
| 38. | cable, wire | cable and wire are synonyms |
| 39. | harm, injure | harm and injure are synonyms |

## Section 10

| Question | Answer | Explanation |
|---|---|---|
| 40. | hive started | vest |
| 41. | rink now | know |
| 42. | aqua yacht | quay |
| 43. | young librarian | glib |
| 44. | teacher explained | here |

## Section 11

| Question | Answer | Explanation |
|---|---|---|
| 45. | YEW | The missing word uses letter three (Y) from the first word and letters two and three (WE) from the second word, and amends the order to create YEW. |
| 46. | NIL | The missing word uses letters two and three (IN) from the first word and letter two (L) from the second word, and amends the order to create NIL. |
| 47. | PACY | The missing word uses letters one and three (CP) from the first word and letters two and three (YA) from the second word, and amends the order to create PACY. |
| 48. | CHIN | The missing word uses letters one and four (CN) from the first word and letters two and four (IH) from the second word, and amends the order to create CHIN. |
| 49. | TUNE | The missing word uses letters two and four (UT) from the first word and letters two and four (EN) from the second word, and amends the order to create TUNE. |
| 50. | PART | The missing word uses letters three and five (AP) from the first word and letters two and three (TR) from the second word, and amends the order to create PART. |
| 51. | VENT | The missing word uses letters two and three (EV) from the first word and letters and letters one and three (NT) from the second word, and amends the order to create VENT. |

## Section 12

| Question | Answer | Explanation |
|---|---|---|
| 52. | 63 | This question uses alternate sequences – the first decreases by 7 each time and the second increases by 7 each time. So the first pattern is 57 to 50 to 43 and the second is 49 to 56 to 63. |
| 53. | 4.93 | The sequence in this question adds 0.01 then 1.00 alternately. |
| 54. | 18 | This question adds 1 then 2, then 3, then 4 and so on. |
| 55. | 3 | The sequence in this question divides by 6 each time. |
| 56. | 102 | This sequence adds an increasing square number each time, so 4, then 9, then 16, then 25 and then 36. |
| 57. | 11 | The sequence in this question adds the previous two numbers to make the next number. |

## Section 13

| Question | Answer | Explanation |
|---|---|---|
| 58. | 16 | To find the relationship you divide the number on the left by the number on the right and then double the answer. |
| 59. | 40 | To find the relationship you add the numbers outside the brackets and then double the answer. |
| 60. | 57 | To find the relationship you multiply the numbers on the outside then add 1. |
| 61. | 28 | To find the relationship you double the number on the right then add it to the number on the left. |
| 62. | 15 | To find the relationship you add the 2 numbers outside the brackets and then divide the answer by 4. |

## Section 14

| Question | Answer | Explanation |
|---|---|---|
| 63. | 61975 | Slept = 25169, lives = 53812, vital = 83975. There are several ways of breaking this code. The number 5 appears in all three number codes in different places. It must be since this is the only letter that starts and ends a word and also appears second in a word. This then gives us the answers above. From these we can work out the answers to the questions using the same code. So with the word petal, we first find a number which matches P. We can find this in the word slept where P = 6; next we look for E which appears in slept and lives and its number is 1. We continue in this way until we have all the numbers and find the answer as 61975. |
| 64. | 29781 | Using the same method and codes as above we start by finding the letter S which starts the word slept and ends the word lives. We can see that it is represented by the number 2; next we look for a T which is at the end of the word slept and in the middle of the word vital. It is represented by the number 9. We continue in this way until we have the whole code which is 29781. |
| 65. | PLATE | To find the answer you need to use the same code as the previous two questions but reverse the process. This time we look for the number 6 which represents the letter P in slept so that's our first letter; next we look for a 5 which ends the word vital and is second in the word slept so 5 = L. We continue in this way until we have all the letters and the answer is plate (6 = P, 5 = L, 7 = A, 9 = T and 1 = E). |

## Section 15

| Question | Answer | Explanation |
|---|---|---|
| 66. | GRAPE | Gleam = 23748, pearl = 17493, stamp = 56481. The number 4 is key for this code as it appears in all three code numbers and must be A as the middle letter. From this we can work out that only GLEAM has A as its fourth letter and this breaks the code. We use this code to see that 29417 means GRAPE (2 = G, 9 = R, 4 = A, 1 = P and 7 = E). |
| 67. | PAGES | Using the same method and code as above we start by looking for the number 1 which appears as the first number in the word pearl and the last number in the word stamp, so 1 = P. We know from the code that 4 = A and so we continue in this way until we have all the letters; 1 = P, 4 = A, 2 = G, 7 = E and 5 = S. |
| 68. | 48137 | We use the same code as the previous two questions but reverse the process. We know that A = 4 so next we look for the letter M which is found in stamp and at the end of gleam – it is represented by the number 8. We continue in this way until we have all the answer: A = 4, M = 8, P = 1, L = 3 and E = 7. |

## Section 16

| Question | Answer | Explanation |
|---|---|---|
| 69. | expand, contract | expand and contract are antonyms |
| 70. | vigour, lethargy | vigour and lethargy are antonyms |
| 71. | ruthless, merciful | ruthless and merciful are antonyms |
| 72. | aggravate, soothe | aggravate and soothe are antonyms |
| 73. | luminous, dark | luminous and dark are antonyms |

## Section 17

| Question | Answer | Explanation |
|---|---|---|
| 74. | rage | To find the missing word you move the first letter so it becomes the third letter. Letters two and three start the word and an 'e' is placed on the end so ra + g + e = rage. |
| 75. | vain | The missing word is created from letters three and four which start the word and is finished by letters one and two. |
| 76. | dirt | To find the missing word you drop the middle two letters. |
| 77. | cats | The missing word is created using letters one, three, five and six in that order. |
| 78. | toe | The missing word is created using letters one, two and four. |

## Section 18

| Question | Answer | Explanation |
|---|---|---|
| 79. | KP | The first letter goes forward two each time and the second letter goes back two each time. |
| 80. | YZ | The pattern for the first letter is going forward five places then four then three, then two for our answer, while the pattern for the second letter is going forward two then three then four and then five for our answer. |
| 81. | SJ | The pattern for the first letter is going back one then two then four, then eight for our answer (amount doubles each time); second letter goes forward, alternating between one and two each time. |
| 82. | JG | The first letter goes back one each time while the second letter is repeated then goes forward two, then is repeated then goes forward two for our answer. |
| 83. | JI | The first letter goes forward one then back three then forward five, then back seven for our answer; second letter goes forward three then back five then forward seven, then back nine for our answer. |
| 84. | HD | The first letter goes back three each time and the second letter goes forward two each time. |
| 85. | PX | The pattern in this question alternates between one and two jumps each time; so the first letter goes back two, then back one and so on, while the second letter goes forward one, then forward two and so on. |

# HOW TO IMPROVE SCORES

Students scoring 60 out of 85 or fewer in each paper may require further practice. There are several ways students can improve upon their initial scores. Here are some more hints and tips to help them achieve a better score.

**TIMINGS**

Often students either struggle to complete all the questions in the time, or they race through and finish with a lot of time to spare. Neither of these situations is ideal.

If your child was not able to finish all of the questions you need to find out why. Ask them to point out any difficult questions which they encountered in the paper and this will be where they have lost time. Encourage them to practise these questions but also encourage them to 'skip' these questions, complete the paper and then return to them at the end. In this way your child will get to see all of the questions and spend enough time on those questions they find easier before tackling the more difficult ones.

If your child is a fast worker, you need to try and slow them down a little. The main reason for this is that you don't want them misreading questions because they are going too fast. Encourage them to underline key words in questions and to look at the examples – where given – so they really understand what to do. On questions involving the alphabet and codes, get them to mark their answers on the alphabet each time then rub out their working ready for the next question. The more they make notes and write things down, the less likely they are to miss vital information.

**FURTHER TIPS**

- Do tell students to write down workings for each question where possible. These will prove invaluable when checking at the end.
- Get students to check they have marked an answer in each answer grid – often students forget to do this for each question or mark them in the wrong order or even mark two on one grid and none on the next.

## MATHEMATICAL-TYPE PROBLEMS

Some questions on verbal reasoning papers now include mathematical-type problems. Some also include letters, similar to some algebra questions. You should make sure your child is prepared for this type of question.

If a question asks students to replace letters with numbers and then solve the problem, students need to know that two letters placed next to each other should be multiplied.

*Example*

Question: If A = 2, B = 3, C = 4, D = 5 and E = 6, what letter represents the answer to CE − CD?

In the question above CE is 4 × 6 (not 46) which equals 24 and CD is 4 × 5 (not 45) which equals 20. So the calculation is 24 − 20 which equals 4.

This means the answer is C.

## FURTHER PRACTICE

It's well worth going over any questions your child got wrong and explaining to them how to get the right answer. If you'd like more questions of a certain type to practise or if you're unsure of the best way to explain a particular question, use this breakdown of where to find different question types in the first two titles in the Practise and Pass series, *Practise & Pass 11+ Level One: Discover Verbal Reasoning* and *Practise & Pass 11+ Level Two: Develop Verbal Reasoning*. That way you can find out how best to explain the questions to them and also give your child lots more practice to help them improve.

*Practice paper 1: question types and further practice references*

| Question | *Practise & Pass 11+ Level One: Discover Verbal Reasoning* lessons to refer to for further practice | *Practise & Pass 11+ Level Two: Develop Verbal Reasoning* lessons to refer to for further practice |
| --- | --- | --- |
| Q1–7 | Lesson 3: Moving a letter to make two new words | Lesson 3: Moving a letter to make two new words |
| Q8–13 | Lesson 13: Replacing letters with numbers to solve an equation | |
| Q14 | | Lesson 10: Solving problems with information |
| Q15–21 | Lesson 1: Finding hidden words | Lesson 1: Finding hidden words |
| Q22–28 | Lesson 15: Finding analogical words | Lesson 15: Finding analogical words |
| Q29–35 | Lesson 7: Finding synonyms | |
| Q36–42 | | Lesson 16: Finding the two words which don't belong in the group |
| Q43–49 | Lesson 2: Filling in the missing three-letter word | Lesson 2: Filling in the missing three-letter word |
| Q50 | | Lesson 10: Solving problems with information |
| Q51–57 | Lesson 9: Working out the missing letters for each sequence | Lesson 9: Working out the missing letters for each sequence |
| Q58–64 | Lesson 6: Forming compound words | Lesson 6: Forming compound words |
| Q65–71 | | Lesson 19: Finding the second word using those outside the brackets |
| Q72–78 | Lesson 12: Completing number patterns | Lesson 12: Completing number patterns |
| Q79–85 | | Lesson 14: Solving coded analogies |

*Practice paper 2: question types and further practice references*

| Question | *Practise & Pass 11+ Level One: Discover Verbal Reasoning* lessons to refer to for further practice | *Practise & Pass 11+ Level Two: Develop Verbal Reasoning* lessons to refer to for further practice |
|---|---|---|
| Q1–7 | Lesson 3: Moving a letter to make two new words | Lesson 3: Moving a letter to make two new words |
| Q8–14 | | Lesson 16: Finding the two words which don't belong in a group |
| Q15–21 | Lesson 13: Replacing letters with numbers to solve an equation | |
| Q22 | | Lesson 10: Solving problems with information |
| Q23–29 | Lesson 15: Finding analogical words | Lesson 15: Finding analogical words |
| Q30–36 | Lesson 6: Forming compound words | Lesson 6: Forming compound words |
| Q37–43 | Lesson 1: Finding hidden words | Lesson 1: Finding hidden words |
| Q44 | | Lesson 10: Solving problems with information |
| Q45–51 | Lesson 2: Filling in the missing three-letter word | Lesson 2: Filling in the missing three-letter word |
| Q52–58 | Lesson 7: Finding synonyms | |
| Q59–65 | Lesson 9: Working out the missing letters for each sequence | Lesson 9: Working out the missing letters for each sequence |
| Q66–72 | | Lesson 19: Finding the second word using those outside the brackets |
| Q73–79 | Lesson 12: Completing number patterns | Lesson 12: Completing number patterns |
| Q80–85 | Lesson 11: Working out indirect codes | Lesson 11: Working out indirect codes |

*Practice paper 3: question types and further practice references*

| Question | *Practise & Pass 11+ Level One: Discover Verbal Reasoning* lessons to refer to for further practice | *Practise & Pass 11+ Level Two: Develop Verbal Reasoning* lessons to refer to for further practice |
| --- | --- | --- |
| Q1–7 | Lesson 3: Moving a letter to make two new words | Lesson 3: Moving a letter to make two new words |
| Q8–14 | | Lesson 16: Finding the two words which don't belong in the group |
| Q15–21 | Lesson 13: Replacing letters with numbers to solve an equation | |
| Q22 | | Lesson 10: Solving problems with information |
| Q23–29 | Lesson 15: Finding analogical words | Lesson 15: Finding analogical words |
| Q30 | | Lesson 10: Solving problems with information |
| Q31–37 | Lesson 6: Forming compound words | Lesson 6: Forming compound words |
| Q38–44 | Lesson 14: Solving coded analogies | Lesson 14: Solving coded analogies |
| Q45–51 | Lesson 2: Filling in the missing three-letter word | Lesson 2: Filling in the missing three-letter word |
| Q52–58 | Lesson 7: Finding synonyms | |
| Q59–65 | Lesson 1: Finding hidden words | Lesson 1: Finding hidden words |
| Q66–72 | | Lesson 19: Finding the second word using those outside the brackets |
| Q73–77 | Lesson 12: Completing number patterns | Lesson 12: Completing number patterns |
| Q78–82 | | Lesson 20: Using the numbers outside the brackets to find the one on the inside |
| Q83–85 | | Lesson 17: Working out the missing codes for each word |

## Practice paper 4: question types and further practice references

| Question | Practise & Pass 11+ Level One: Discover Verbal Reasoning lessons to refer to for further practice | Practise & Pass 11+ Level Two: Develop Verbal Reasoning lessons to refer to for further practice |
|---|---|---|
| Q1–7 | | Lesson 16: Finding the two words which don't belong in the group |
| Q8–12 | Lesson 13: Replacing letters with numbers to solve an equation | |
| Q13 | | Lesson 10: Solving problems with information |
| Q14–18 | Lesson 15: Finding analogical words | Lesson 15: Finding analogical words |
| Q19 | | Lesson 10: Solving problems with information |
| Q20–24 | Lesson 6: Forming compound words | Lesson 6: Forming compound words |
| Q25–29 | Lesson 14: Solving coded analogies | Lesson 14: Solving coded analogies |
| Q30–34 | Lesson 2: Filling in the missing three-letter word | Lesson 2: Filling in the missing three-letter word |
| Q35–39 | Lesson 7: Finding synonyms | |
| Q40–44 | Lesson 1: Finding hidden words | Lesson 1: Finding hidden words |
| Q45–51 | | Lesson 19: Finding the second word using those outside the brackets |
| Q52–57 | Lesson 12: Completing number patterns | Lesson 12: Completing number patterns |
| Q58–62 | | Lesson 20: Using the numbers outside the brackets to find those on the inside |
| Q63–68 | | Lesson 17: Working out the missing codes for each word |
| Q69–73 | | Lesson 7: Finding opposites |
| Q74–78 | | Lesson 18: Completing the third pair of words using the same pattern |
| Q79–85 | Lesson 9: Working out the missing letters for each sequence | Lesson 9: Working out the missing letters for each sequence |